"*From Broken Vows to Healed Hearts* sensitively addresses the pain of divorce and offers practical steps toward healing. Rebecca Mitchell's voice is honest, relatable, and encouraging. Readers will find comfort and hope as they follow her gentle pathway through Bible study, prayer, and reflection." —Susan A. Reynolds, marriage and family therapist

"Comforting, challenging, and spiritually rich, this devotional provides a window for reflection and a hopeful path toward healing and restoration. Its practical illustrations and wise insights drawn from experience make this a powerful resource for finding and growing in God's grace during tough times." —The Rev. Dr. Roberta Hestenes, teaching pastor at Bayside Church and former president of Eastern University

"Mitchell's insights invite women to the identity that God gives them as His beloved, which no circumstances, not even divorce, can alter. My favorite parts are the love letters from God at the beginnings of each chapter, written in the style of *Jesus Calling*." —Deb Gruelle, chaplain for Inspire Christian Writers and author of *The Ache for a Child*

"Heartfelt and inspiring, *From Broken Vows to Healed Hearts* shows us that even in darkness our light still shines. Rebecca Mitchell illuminates the ever-present power of God in our lives and the blessed gift of finding Him, and ourselves, through our journeys of struggle and despair. Mitchell's writing is beautiful and gentle, connecting with those in all stages of divorce. Her prayers set this devotional apart, saying for us what we can't articulate in our pain and grief." —Chandra E. Miller, lawyer

"*From Broken Vows to Healed Hearts* is a prescription for healing. Rebecca has taken the truth of God's Word, which leads and heals, and applied it both practically and personally. If you are living with a broken heart, this method of being open to God through meditation, prayer, and journaling will allow Him to bring restoration." —Cheryl Bangs, lead associate pastor at Bayside Church of Citrus Heights

"*From Broken Vows to Healed Hearts* beautifully illustrates the compassionate heart of God. Nobody writes about this topic with as much wisdom as Rebecca Mitchell. A labor of love and courage, this book is an extraordinary gift to everyone grappling with divorce. It is my prayer that God's words will come alive in you as you read these pages and your wounds become 'beauty for ashes.'" —Elizabeth Min Hui Kim, MD, MPH, FACS, surgical oncologist

"Women do not have to go through the difficult journey of divorce alone: They can turn first to God, and He can transform their feelings of hopelessness into the healing and restoration of their hearts. And they can get support and encouragement from others who are traveling the same path to healing. Readers will discover not only that they can survive but that they can grow closer to God, establish a vision for their future, and thrive in the new life they create." —Susan Markley, Divorce Care program facilitator at Bayside Church, Granite Bay Campus

"Rebecca tells her story courageously while delivering what every reader who's been through a divorce needs: hope and restoration. Whether you're facilitating a Bible study or reading on your own, *From Broken Vows to Healed Hearts* is the book I would recommend. The thought-provoking questions, beautiful letters, and journaling opportunities will accelerate you on your journey to healing." —Jodie Stevens, radio host of *Genuine Life* and the *Fish Family Morning Show*

"Rebecca's powerful voice of compassion, humor, and raw emotion wrap up a package of hope. I wholeheartedly recommend this book to leaders, groups, and individuals who choose to look in the mirror. Looking in the mirror to own our challenges, growth, and healing is a choice. Let Rebecca's heart and mind lead you past the broken moments into the joy of today." —April Ballestero, strategic leadership coach and owner of One Light Ahead

FROM
Broken Vows
TO
Healed
Hearts

SEEKING GOD AFTER DIVORCE
THROUGH COMMUNITY, SCRIPTURE, AND JOURNALING

REBECCA L. MITCHELL

From Broken Vows to Healed Hearts: Seeking God After Divorce Through Community, Scripture, and Journaling
© 2018 by Rebecca L. Mitchell

Published by Kregel Publications, a division of Kregel Inc., 2450 Oak Industrial Dr. NE, Grand Rapids, MI 49505.

The author and publisher are not engaged in rendering medical or psychological services, and this book is not intended as a guide to diagnose or treat medical or psychological problems. If medical, psychological, or other expert assistance is required, the reader should seek the services of a healthcare provider or certified counselor.

Scripture quotations are from the Holy Bible, New International Version®, NIV®. Copyright © 1973, 1978, 1984, 2011 by Biblica, Inc.™ Used by permission of Zondervan. All rights reserved worldwide. www.zondervan.com

ISBN 978-0-8254-4523-1

Printed in the United States of America
18 19 20 21 22 23 24 25 26 27 / 5 4 3 2 1

To my daughters, Meghan and McKenzie,
for making me laugh,
for loving me as I am,
and for just being you.
I love you!

Contents

Dear Reader

Welcome! Words cannot fully convey the heart-wrenching despair that occurs when a marriage ends, whether through divorce or death. We feel devastation, rejection, fear, heartbreak, grief, guilt, confusion, doubt, anger, self-condemnation—the list could go on and on. For some of us, this is the worst experience of our lives, and we wonder how we will make it to the next day, let alone the next year.

Facing the reality of our current situation and our unknown future often feels overwhelming, even hopeless. While we are hurting, the enemy would like us to stay focused on our circumstances, and he wears us down to the point of despair by filling our heads with lies about ourselves (*I'm too weak to recover from this; I'm ugly and unlovable*) and about God (*God wants to punish me for my past life; God doesn't care and isn't even listening to my prayers*).

In John 5, Jesus asks a surprising question of the man hoping to enter a pool of water with healing powers. This man has been an invalid for thirty-eight years, and Jesus asks him, "Do you want to get well?" The answer seems obvious, but perhaps Jesus asks him to shift his focus off his circumstances—he had no one to help him—and off the pool of water, in order to recognize Jesus as the source of power to heal him. Jesus heals the man in an instant.

While we yearn for an instantaneous cure, for an immediate end to our pain, our healing will likely consist of a long, arduous journey. Fortunately, this is not a solitary endeavor. In fact, I believe we cannot carry on alone, at least not well. I once voiced my opinion about this need for community to my therapist, who concurred, saying, "Is there any other way?" God has designed us to seek intimacy, support, comfort, guidance, and strength from Him and friends and family.

During the early stages of my separation and divorce, I relied heavily on several support groups, including Divorce Care, a worldwide divorce recovery support program. (See appendix E for more information about recovery support groups.) After I made progress in my own healing and began to write, God impressed upon me the need for more opportunities for women to support each other as they go through this devastating experience.

Often we feel cast adrift and utterly alone in our heartache, and we need to meet with a small, intimate group of women going through similar turmoil. As a result, I began a small-group Bible study for women, using this material.

My prayer for the women meeting in my home and for you—whether you are meeting with others or reading individually—is that in our Lord's loving arms, we find love, healing, peace, and strength not merely to survive but to thrive.

To that end, I invite you to read my story, knowing God is creating a story in you as well.

May God bless and heal you through your new story.

Rebecca

Introduction

I call the last three years of my marriage the dark years, as I struggled simply to function amid the chaos and turmoil that had entered my home. Our covenant had been broken, and despite sincere prayer and effort, our marriage was not restored. I was shocked and devastated. My best friend, the father of my children, the person I had expected to grow old with, had moved on. Shortly after our twenty-fifth wedding anniversary, which we did not celebrate, I finally faced the reality of the demise of our marriage, and we separated. We were legally divorced in November 2014.

The dark years, without question, were the most difficult of my life—the details of which I am intentionally omitting for the sake of privacy. I have discovered the fruitlessness of rehashing the past; it only derails me from my journey forward toward healing. When I instead *reflect* on the past, I see evidence that God is good and has walked through this dark valley with me, providing comfort through His unconditional love, faithfulness, and strength. I have been brokenhearted, but I am mending with help from God's healing love, supportive family, and wonderful friends.

Looking back, I can see my progression—and sometimes regression—through the following stages:

Stage 1: I can't believe this is happening to me!
Stage 2: I'm so angry I could _____!
Stage 3: When will this pain ever go away?

Stage 4: I don't feel good, but I do feel better.

Stage 5: I have a new life, and I can find joy in it.

Much of my personal journey has been a battle to emerge from the pain stage to experience true and lasting healing. I became emotionally weary of crying, hurting, feeling sorry for myself, and rehashing the past. I wanted to move forward. I wanted to stop talking about what happened *to* me. I wanted to focus on growth, identity, and a new hope for the future.

While this shift in focus has not been easy or speedy, it has been worth it! My journey has taught me to maintain hope for healing, to be patient with the process, to be committed to community, and above all, to seek God.

I feel compelled to share what I have learned and am still learning in the hope that it will bring comfort to others. I hope that this devotional meets you in your brokenness and gently moves you through the above stages to healing. While my personal experience centers around divorce, my widowed friends assure me that their experiences of loss, grief, fear, and recovery are very similar to my own. My prayer is that through this book, we commit to a journey of healing together and "grasp how wide and long and high and deep is the love of Christ" (Eph. 3:18).

Getting the Most out of This Book

The topics in each chapter cover common feelings and experiences during and after the loss of a marriage. The early chapters on brokenness, depression, and loneliness discuss the devastation we feel in those initial traumatic days. The next chapters on helplessness, fear, guilt, and forgiveness capture our struggles as we begin to face our new reality as single women. The last chapters—dealing with hope, identity, intimacy, and joy—offer a shift to the promise of restoration and healing.

Each chapter has many Bible verses. If you are not familiar with the Bible or are not sure where you stand with God, please know that previous Bible knowledge is not necessary, and God knows and accepts us exactly where we are today. If at any point during your reading and journaling you would like to begin or renew your relationship with God, please see appendix B.

Chapter Structure

Each chapter consists of five entries, labeled Day 1 through Day 5. Day 1 introduces the psalm of the week to read and has a section called "Seeing God's Heart." This section contains a letter to you from God's point of view, to serve as a reminder that He intimately knows and understands your pain and longs to provide comfort and counsel. Days 2 through 4 begin with reading suggestions for the same psalm and include devotionals called "Seeking God First." These devotionals usually begin with a brief story and end with a spiritual application, to help you seek God first as you progress in your healing journey. Day 5 invites you to focus on one passage in the Bible and helps you find hope for healing in the stories there.

If you're in a group study, your leader will let you know whether you should do the Day 5 study ahead of your meeting. Since studies show that journaling promotes healing, each day has thoughtful journaling questions. If you don't have a journal, consider purchasing one before beginning the first week. The last chapter, "Seeking God for Our Next Steps," offers the same format, plus suggestions and resources for your next steps.

Reading the Psalms

Psalms are musical poems especially appropriate to read and meditate on when going through emotionally challenging times. As you read the psalms, reflect on the psalmists' heartfelt emotions and thoughts regarding their circumstances, desires, and understanding of God. Try to read the psalm of the week every day and ask God for insight. The Word of God is alive, and you may see new truths each time you read the psalm, especially during these emotionally tumultuous times. Some directions are given, such as reading it out loud or circling certain words, to help you focus your attention on the reading for that day. You may also want to memorize your favorite verse and remind yourself of specific passages by, for example, placing portions of the psalm on your bathroom mirror.

Group or Individual Study

You can use this resource on your own, with one friend, or with a group of other women experiencing the same loss. If meeting in a group—either in person or online—you can convey what God has taught you during the week, study the Bible passage together, and share your prayer needs. (See rebeccamitchellauthor.com for a free download of the leader's guide.) Resist the temptation to isolate, and instead seek help in community. Support from others is invaluable during this difficult time. (See appendix A for group guidelines that will help you create a safe space for healing.)

Warning!

Reading and journaling about these heavy topics five days a week can easily become overwhelming, especially when you are in the deer-in-the-headlights survival stage. If you feel this way, try some of the following suggestions:

- Skim the entries—or part of the entries such as the questions—to see which ones resonate more with you. Choose one or two to focus on that week.
- Read each day's entry but only journal as you have time or inclination.
- Read the first two entries each week as you proceed through the book. After you finish the entire book, return to the beginning and read the next two entries, and so on.
- Again, if you are going through this book with others in a group, save Day 5, the Bible study, for when you meet together.

Let the Holy Spirit guide your reading and responses. God can speak to you in your journaling time to bring wisdom and comfort in His presence. Also, looking back through your journal is helpful for noticing patterns, answered prayer, and areas of growth.

Unfortunately, even after thoroughly tackling every topic with reading, journaling, prayer, and Bible study, some issues will resurface. Something may trigger our loneliness or anger, for example, and we will take a step or two backward. The good news is that we will recover more quickly than before, and with the help of God and others, we will continue to move forward in our healing journey. (For ideas and resources for continuing to move forward, see appendixes C through E.)

Setting Expectations

During this time, we all easily become overly critical as we look inward. We beat ourselves up, replay regrets, or retreat in despair. We might also compare ourselves to others, resulting in further self-condemnation, jealousy, depression, or pride. God loves us exactly as we are today. Period. Philip Yancey beautifully connects this unconditional love and acceptance to God's grace: *"Grace means there is nothing we can do to make God love us more . . . And grace means there is nothing we can do to make God love us less."*[1]

Satan is not pleased with our work toward healing and a closer relationship with God. Expect some attacks, including circumstances and feelings that might tempt you to give up or find a counterfeit solution to escape your pain. On the other hand, realize that God is pleased with your decision to move forward and longs to bring healing to your heart. Moving closer to God and healing is hard work. It is also holy work. Expect God's blessings and presence, perhaps in ways you have never known before.

PART I

The Initial Devastation

Chapter 1

Seeking God in Our Brokenness

Psalm of the Week: Psalm 34

Day 1

FINDING HEALING IN PSALM 34
Read Psalm 34. Look for verses that reveal
God's heart for hurting people.

Seeing God's Heart

My beautiful daughter,

I know you feel broken, shattered beyond repair. The pain seems relentless, the fear overwhelming, the guilt consuming. You can hardly breathe, barely function at times, as if walking aimlessly in a daze, still in shock at this unforeseen turmoil that has completely upended your life. You wonder if you will ever recover. You wonder if you will ever feel normal again.

I know this path is not what you expected or would have chosen, but please have ears to hear. This path will not bring you to ruin. You can survive, endure, even thrive because My grace is sufficient for you. I love you unconditionally, so take one day at a time and draw close to Me.

Cry out to Me. I am always listening.

Take refuge in Me. I will deliver you from your fears.

Look to Me. I will bless you and remove your shame.

Seek Me. I am close to the brokenhearted.

Remember I have restored whole nations to Me. I am willing and able to heal you and make you whole. I have made you, and I will carry you; I will sustain you, and I will rescue you. I love you!

Your loving Father

Talking to God

"Father God, I am so overwhelmed, I don't even know how to pray. I just know I am broken, and I need help even to function. Please teach me how to depend on your strength, goodness, and love to get through the day."

Journaling with God

Which part of the letter most resonates with me and why?

Which invitation is the most challenging for me? Which brings the most comfort?

What does Psalm 34 say about God's help in my brokenness? In what ways is this consistent or inconsistent with my view of God during this time?

FINDING HEALING IN PSALM 34

Read Psalm 34. Underline all the verbs that show God's active help in our lives. For example, in verse 4, the verbs are *answered* and *delivered*.

Seeking God First—Broken Vases

[God bestows] on them a crown of beauty instead of ashes.
(Isa. 61:3)

A rock hit my windshield. I didn't repair it right away, and what was once a circular chip smaller than a dime is now an L-shaped crack twelve inches long. Although my passengers might stare at the eye-level flaw in irritation, I ignore it, waiting for my next financial windfall to pay for the repair. It's been over a year. Besides, I think my Toyota will never be quite the same once I break that factory seal.

Often when something breaks, if it's not too expensive, we simply throw it away. If it is repairable, we may make the effort to fix it, expecting it will still be useful but never quite the same. We make do with the repaired item, perhaps hiding its flaws, until we can afford to replace it.

The art of *kintsugi* deals with brokenness differently.

Kintsugi is the Japanese art of mending broken pottery. Resin is mixed with gold dust and then applied to the broken pottery to hold the pieces together. What was once a ruined vase, a pile of broken pieces, is restored with veins of gold and becomes a stunning work of art. The breakage is not ignored or hidden—it is illuminated and accentuated. The restoration and subsequent repair of the pottery becomes part of the history of the piece, which enhances rather than diminishes its usefulness and beauty.

We feel broken, even shattered, after the loss of a marriage. We see ourselves as failures—rejected, lost, and hopeless. Even if our open wounds have healed, we hardly think of scars from the wounds as veins of gold that make us more useful and beautiful than before. But that is exactly how God sees us and how we can come to see ourselves. God is a patient kintsugi artist, who mends broken pieces into masterpieces and turns our shame into radiance. We become a visual representation of God's restorative power. As we heal, we gain a deeper understanding of who He is, how great His love for us is, and how we can help others experience His love.

Yes, we look different. Being broken was not part of the original plan. But God can heal and restore us to an abundant, joy-filled life as we walk closely with Him. What could be more beautiful?

_____

I praise you because I am fearfully and wonderfully made; your works are wonderful, I know that full well. (Ps. 139:14)

Talking to God

"Lord, my circumstances devastate me. I feel broken and anything but beautiful, and I wonder if I can ever be whole again. Help me to believe and expect your healing power in my life. Help me to see myself as You see me."

Journaling with God

In what ways do I feel broken today?

How do I think God sees me? What does Psalm 34 say about how God sees me?

What can I do to help me see myself as useful and beautiful, like God sees me?

FINDING HEALING IN PSALM 34

Read Psalm 34, and focus on verses 17 and 18. Copy these verses and place them in an easily visible location, so you can see them throughout the day.

Seeking God First—Demo Day

There is a time for everything . . . a time to tear down and a time to build. (Eccl. 3:1, 3)

The popcorn ceiling visibly sagged, the avocado green carpet smelled of mildew and moth balls, and the kitchen had no appliances but plenty of cockroaches. The clients bought the house anyway. Why? Because they had hired expert renovators Chip and Joanna Gaines from the popular TV show *Fixer Upper*.

At the beginning of the renovation, Chip can hardly contain his enthusiasm for demolition day, affectionately known as Demo Day. Before they can create the dream home, they have to remove every unwanted thing. Chip rips out worn and outdated cabinets, counters, and carpet. He removes old appliances, ugly wallpaper, and ancient light fixtures. He even destroys walls to create sight lines for the highly popular open concept the new homeowners desire.

The challenge with Demo Day is that previously hidden and unaddressed problems—wiring not up to code, water damage, unsupported walls, hornet nests—come to light. Chip and Joanna can't ignore these serious issues; they must address them before they can make structurally sound and safe progress.

We may feel as though we've been the object of Demo Day when we are stripped of everything we once thought of as normal, secure, purposeful. Then, staggering under the exposure of the brokenness in our marriage and in ourselves, we become overwhelmed with the task of restoring and rebuilding our lives apart from our spouse and may feel that "the house" should just be razed to the ground. But, carrying the metaphor further, Chip and Joanna will often say the house has good bones and occasionally they find hidden treasures, such as shiplap, wooden floors, or even a message in a bottle left by a previous owner decades before.

Although painful, Demo Day can be good for us. God creates clear, straight sight lines to Him, to our other relationships, and even to ourselves, so we can better understand and recover from our brokenness. We are stripped to bare essentials to enable us to visualize what is important and what we need to do to become stronger and better. We also have the opportunity to expose and demolish old wounds that we have tolerated for many years. Current struggles often bring to light past distresses that we have ignored, either intentionally or unintentionally. Hopefully, we can honestly examine the state of our house and be willing to endure the pain of removing the old for the joy of the new. In her book *Dancing in the Arms of God*, Connie Neal describes this process of recovering from enormous devastation: "As I let myself grieve my losses, deeper losses and leftover pain from the past resurfaced. God could then heal the deep hurts that I hadn't been able to see."[2]

The LORD is close to the brokenhearted and saves those who are crushed in spirit. (Ps. 34:18)

Talking to God

"Lord, I confess that I don't want to face my brokenness. I want to pretend my house is in order, but I can't anymore. I invite You to expose my denial, my hidden brokenness. Help me to be willing to do the hard work of tearing away what is broken and to trust You to restore me in ways I cannot even imagine right now."

Journaling with God

In what ways have I already experienced Demo Day?

What deeper wounds, if any, have surfaced during this time?

What fears do I have about facing these deeper wounds?

How can God help me understand and heal from these deep wounds?

FINDING HEALING IN PSALM 34

Read Psalm 34. Underline the verbs that describe the actions of a person seeking God. (For example, the verb in verse 5 is *look* and the verb in verse 6 is *called*.)

Seeking God First—Growing Pains

My comfort in my suffering is this: your promise preserves my life.
(Ps. 119:50)

Although my student was a high school athlete, young and strong, her recovery from back surgery was more difficult than expected. She learned some tough life lessons as she battled with the pain. A previously active cheerleader and water polo player, she was eager to return to her activities but knew it would take a while for her body to heal. She figured that she could participate again once the pain went away.

Soon, however, she learned that she couldn't wait until she was completely pain-free to resume her normal activities. Yes, she had to begin slowly to avoid reinjury, but if she didn't move at all, her muscles would tighten up, and she would end up in even worse pain and diminish or even eradicate the benefits of the surgery altogether.

Of course divorce is painful. There are times when we don't want to move because we can't bear more pain. We can't imagine one more step, one more day. I spent many, many hours lying in bed, crying and listening to breakup songs such as "Stop Draggin' My Heart Around," "We Are Never Ever Getting Back Together," and "Harden My Heart."

At best, it was okay to face the grief in that way for a season, but then I needed to get out of bed. I needed to move—at least a little bit—even though it was still painful. My first small step was to change my playlist to songs of hope and healing such as "A Little Bit Stronger," "Need You Now," and "Cry Out to Jesus," with positive lyrics for my soul. Instead of fretting about what's way down the road, I gradually learned to make choices that would help me for that moment, for that day. Should I call somebody? Go for a walk? Spend time with my girls? Make time for myself?

We may feel frozen initially, but we can eventually learn to rely on God's provision of strength and courage to move in the midst of pain.

Again the one who looked like a man touched me and gave me strength. "Do not be afraid, you who are highly esteemed," he said. "Peace! Be strong now; be strong." (Dan. 10:18–19)

Talking to God

"Lord, You know I am sometimes overwhelmed by pain and can't move. I am afraid my pain will just get worse. Please give me the strength to seek healing and the wisdom to know the steps to take to get moving. I trust You to be not only my catalyst but also my ever-present support along the way."

Journaling with God

On a scale from one to ten, what is my level of pain today?

Do I believe God understands and is sensitive to my pain?

What are some healthy and unhealthy ways I deal with my pain?

What step does God want me to take today to reduce my level of pain?

Finding Hope in Naomi's Story (Ruth 1)

Sometimes we think the Bible's stories consist of spiritual giants, far superior to us. On the contrary, the Bible is alive with people just like us who struggle, make mistakes, feel despair, and desperately need help in times of hardship. They were broken too. We can learn from their imperfect reactions to their circumstances and take comfort from God's merciful responses.

Because of a famine in Israel, Naomi, with her husband and two sons, left Bethlehem and moved to Moab, a foreign country that provided food for her family. Although the Moabites did not share Naomi's faith in God, Naomi lived peacefully there for ten years. This peace did not last, however, and Naomi returned to Israel a broken woman.

Read what happened to Naomi in Ruth 1:1–13.

My Brokenness

What words or phrases come to mind when you think of the word *brokenness*? What visual image do you see?

Dictionary.com defines broken as "reduced to fragments, ruptured, torn, or not functioning properly." In what ways does this definition fit you? On a scale from one to ten, how broken do you feel today?

Naomi's Brokenness

What losses did Naomi experience, and in what ways might she have felt broken because of these losses?

How did she feel toward God in these circumstances?

What else do you learn about Naomi's circumstances and her feelings in Ruth 1?

In what ways do you relate to Naomi?

Psalm 34:18 says, "The LORD is close to the brokenhearted and saves those who are crushed in spirit." In what ways is this verse true for Naomi?

Although these questions cover only the first chapter in Ruth, you can read the rest of the book to see how God redeems Ruth and Naomi, giving them great joy and a new life.

What is most hopeful to you about Naomi's story?

Chapter 2

Seeking God in Our Depression and Grief

Psalm of the Week: Psalm 42

Day 1

FINDING HEALING IN PSALM 42
Read Psalm 42 out loud and note repeated phrases depicting the writer's desperate emotional turmoil.

Seeing God's Heart

My tender child,

You have endured a number of devastating losses, and I feel the pain that stabs at your heart and immobilizes you. Your emotional injuries, both self-inflicted and other-inflicted, feel overwhelming, too heavy to bear. At times, this can easily lead to feelings of depression. Even knowing Me personally and putting your hope in Me does not always make you immune to feeling downcast deep in your soul.

I know the pain you feel. I understand the deep sorrow, debilitating sadness, and desire to give up that you feel on some days. It may sometimes feel to you that I'm distant, as though I've forgotten you, but that isn't true. I'm here to love you and to help you. Bring your pain and your sorrow to me and lay them at My feet. Ask Me for strength for each day, and rest in My unconditional love for you.

Remember that grieving a loss takes time. Don't expect too much of yourself in too short a time. Believe that I have more patience with you than you have with yourself. Also, remember that I don't compare you to any other women, expecting behavior more like theirs. Just because you are feeling this sadness, even for a long time, doesn't mean you are doing anything wrong or that I am disappointed in you.

Draw near to Me as the grief takes its course. Know that I love you, whether you stay in bed all day and cry or keep so busy you don't have time to cry. And I love you when you let the grief come, process it, and then let it go.

Your loving heavenly Father

Talking to God

"Father God, thank You for understanding my sadness. Some days I can't seem to shake it, and then I do nothing and feel worthless. Teach me to rely on You to lift me up from this darkness. I know there are lighter days ahead."

Journaling with God

What strikes me about God's understanding in this letter?

What emotions do I relate to in the letter or in Psalm 42?

This week I give myself permission to _____.

In what ways can I be more patient with myself during this time of loss?

FINDING HEALING IN PSALM 42

Read Psalm 42 and note what comforts the writer of the psalm.

Seeking God First—A Cool Breeze

May your unfailing love be my comfort. (Ps. 119:76)

Every Saturday morning, I ride my bicycle, a seven-speed, sage-green Townie with flat-pedal technology. I imagine myself strong and athletic as I attack a hill, eyes determined, muscles engaged, but I probably look awkward and old, eyes bulged, muscles strained. Onlookers might even be poised to dial 911. That's okay. I can't recapture my athletic youth, but on a still day, I can ride fast enough to create a breeze where none exists. How I appear on my bike is no longer important as that cool breeze refreshes and invigorates me.

When I feel depressed about my situation in life, it is like I am sitting on my bike in the hot, dusty garage. Instead of refreshing, the air is still and stagnant, even suffocating. Depression is very difficult to overcome, and the well-intentioned advice to "snap out of it" is more discouraging than helpful. This is especially true if we have a clinical diagnosis of depression, which is more severe than a season of sadness. However, I do believe we can take steps to alleviate the depression so that one evening we will realize we have an ounce more joy than sadness. We may be surrounded by stress, anger, chaos, grief, worry, and regrets, but God can be the breeze that restores our souls. His love and comfort can swirl around and envelop us with reassurance and hope.

We sometimes have to make the effort to do a bit of pedaling to feel God's breeze. Small steps of action can create that breeze. Draw close to Him. Memorize Scripture. Meditate on His promises. Remember His faithfulness. Pray.

Not all uplifting actions have to be spiritual in nature. Listen to your favorite music. Spend time with friends, maybe even listening and dancing to that favorite music. Get your nails done. Enjoy a nature hike. Go for a bike ride!

———

Why, my soul, are you downcast? Why so disturbed within me?
Put your hope in God, for I will yet praise him, my Savior and
my God. (Ps. 42:5)

Talking to God

"Lord, sometimes it's hard to believe I can ever emerge from the dead stillness around me, so help me to seek opportunities to experience the breeze of Your healing touch in my life. Help me to trust that You can bring refreshment and restoration to my soul. I know that is Your will for me."

Journaling with God

How much am I struggling with depression today? This month? How does this depression affect me?

What new action can I take this week to allow God to create a restorative breeze in my life?

What, if anything, am I doing that blocks God's restorative breeze?

FINDING HEALING IN PSALM 42

Read Psalm 42 and consider what the writer does even though his soul is downcast (see vv. 2, 4–5).

Seeking God First—Highlights

The LORD is good to those whose hope is in him, to the one who seeks him. (Lam. 3:25)

New haircuts mark change. Hair is an integral part of our identity, so when our identity goes through a radical metamorphosis, so might our hair. We shed the old self and reinvent a new one that is better suited for the transformative journey ahead.

Without even being aware of this pattern, I followed it. After I separated from my husband, I cut my hair short and started experimenting with color and highlights. Don't think a buzz cut or purple highlights—my level of experimentation is pretty mild. I decided to cut off about six inches, get layers, and try highlights, which I had never had before.

My stylist completed the tedious process of applying goo and foil to my hair to replace my free gray highlights with lovely—and expensive—golden ones. Then she sat me in a chair with an attached dryer to let the bleaching goo do its magic. After tucking stray strands of hair back into place and making sure I didn't need anything, she walked back to the breakroom, out of sight.

Umm. The dryer? What about the dryer? Thinking she had forgotten to put the dryer on me, in my usual cooperative and compliant nature, I put the dryer on myself without bothering to ask her. Big mistake. It turns out that the heat speeds up the highlighting process, and by the time she discovered me under the dryer, my highlights were more like white road lines instead of kisses from the sun. She fixed it with toner, but I detected a distinct vibe of frustration that I had doubted her expertise and inadvertently foiled her work.

I learned two lessons that day—to not rush the process and to trust the maker of the process.

Healing from a broken relationship, as the proverbial adage "two steps forward, one step back" implies, is slow and painful. We might be like Habakkuk, who lamented, "How long, LORD, must I call for help, but you do not listen?" (Hab. 1:2) or the psalmist who cried out, "My tears have been my food day and night" (Ps. 42:3).

Will this pain ever go away or even shift to a dull ache? Will the sight of couples ever stop producing a stab of loneliness in my heart? Will I ever stop crying? The answer is yes to all, but not as quickly as I want. Although the healing process is slow, God attentively listens to and answers our calls for help.

———

*God is our refuge and strength, an ever-present help
in trouble. (Ps. 46:1)*

Talking to God

"Lord, help me be patient with myself, with circumstances, and with You as I go through this healing process. Help me remember that complete healing is according to Your good and perfect will. You desire the best for me, and I can trust You throughout this healing journey."

Journaling with God

In what areas of this healing process do I need to be more patient?

In what ways have I rushed the process or expected change to happen too quickly? What was the result?

How can I increase my trust in the Lord during this healing journey?

FINDING HEALING IN PSALM 42

Read Psalm 42 and circle the most hopeful or encouraging verse.
Memorize the verse and repeat it out loud as you battle despairing
thoughts and emotions.

Seeking God First—Fainting Spell

You, LORD, hear the desire of the afflicted;
you encourage them, and you listen to their cry,
defending the fatherless and the oppressed.
(Ps. 10:17–18)

My older daughter, Meghan, has trypanophobia. This isn't as bad as it
sounds, and she actually hasn't been clinically diagnosed. Trypanophobia
is an extreme fear of needles and injections. Meghan's symptoms include
increased heart rate, sweaty palms, and dizziness, typical of anybody who
hates needles and not necessarily worthy of the phobia label.

This fear has followed her into adulthood, so one day, my younger
daughter, McKenzie, and I accompanied Meghan for moral support when
she got her blood drawn. Meghan sat in the chair, pale and breathing
rapidly, while McKenzie and I hovered nearby. Meghan's blood was deftly
drawn without incident, but she was still pale and in danger of fainting,
so I held her hand and talked to her, trying to discourage her from getting up too soon. McKenzie said she was thirsty and needed water, but I
told her just to wait a few more minutes and we could all leave together.
Then McKenzie seemed to push me, and as I turned to her in irritation,
down she went! McKenzie, not Meghan, had fainted! I was so intent on
preventing harm to one daughter that I couldn't react quickly enough to
catch the other daughter before she fell.

We can never be perfect parents, especially in the midst of difficult
times such as divorce. The harsh reality is that children will not emerge

unscathed. Certainly we should attempt to minimize the damage, but sometimes, despite our best efforts, we can't stop the fall.

Facing the reality of a broken family and seeing the effect on my girls has caused me deep grief, sometimes leading to periods of depression. My marriage fell into darkness; I fell into darkness; I wanted to protect my children from falling too, but I couldn't—I can't. Still today I wonder how things might be different in their lives if we had been healthier, united parents, and I am deeply saddened by the scars and wounds that remain.

However, I have to move out of my sadness to pick them up and to love them unconditionally. And I can ask for forgiveness for when I was less able to help them in the midst of my own pain.

God continually reminds me of two things: (1) There are no perfect parents, even in healthy marriages, and (2) He loves my daughters even more than I do. I understand this more deeply when I change the pronouns from *you* to *them* in the following verse:

———

So do not fear, for I am with [them]; do not be dismayed, for I am [their] God. I will strengthen [them] and help [them]; I will uphold [them] with my righteous right hand. (Isa. 41:10)

Talking to God

"Forgive me for the mistakes I have made with my children. Help me to remember that You have the power and love to guide and care for them better than I do. You love them even more than I do. I release them to Your care, knowing that You will have a story of redemption for them as well."

Journaling with God

If you have children, answer these questions:

What concerns for my children weigh heaviest upon me?

Do I need to ask for forgiveness and free myself from the guilt of mistakes with my children? How does this guilt influence my emotions?

In what ways can I give my children up to God and trust Him with their lives?

If you do not have children, answer these questions:

What mistakes in my marriage do I most regret?

What close relationships have been affected by my divorce? How does that affect me emotionally?

In what ways is God challenging me to accept forgiveness and let go of my guilt?

Finding Hope in Elijah's Story (1 Kings 19)

This study examines one episode in the life of Elijah, one of God's most well-known and powerful prophets, who received a death threat from King Ahab's wife, Jezebel. The passage does not include the word *depressed*, but it does describe him as such. He escapes to a cave, spends his days sleeping, and can barely eat—all symptoms of depression.

Before his escape to the cave, Elijah had been actively proclaiming God's truth to Ahab, the King of Israel. However, Ahab did not listen and "did more evil in the eyes of the Lord than any of those before him" (1 Kings 16:30), including worshipping other gods, primarily Baal, and having Israel's prophets killed. His wife, Jezebel, also worshipped Baal, and consequently, she hated Elijah.

Elijah goes to Ahab and proposes a contest to determine who the one true God is. Ahab prepares an altar for Baal, and Elijah prepares an altar for the God of Israel. The god who lights his altar on fire would prove to be the one true god. Ahab and four hundred and fifty Baal prophets (and four hundred others) compete against the solitary prophet Elijah and God. The Baal prophets pray, dance, and shout for hours, but nothing happens.

Then it's Elijah's turn. He drenches God's altar with water three times, prays once, and then the altar is instantly aflame. Afterward, Elijah prays for rain after a drought of three years, and again, God answers his prayer. Finally, perhaps in hopeful anticipation of witnessing a declaration from Ahab to follow the God of Israel, Elijah runs down the mountain on foot with God's strength, beating Ahab in his chariot.

Elijah had performed three very powerful and public miracles—and then he hides in a cave, wishing God would take his life. Pay special attention to how God responds to Elijah as you read 1 Kings 19 before answering the following questions.

If you were Elijah, what might you be expecting, thinking, and feeling after the miracles that proved God's existence and power?

After hearing of Jezebel's response (vv. 1–2), what might you be thinking and feeling?

What seems normal and what seems surprising about Elijah's response to Jezebel's message in verses 3 through 5?

After reading verses 5 through 9, what stands out to you about how God responds to Elijah?

What observations and questions do you have about the conversation between God and Elijah in verses 9 through 18?

How might God respond to you when you want to give up and hide in a cave?

Chapter 3

Seeking God in Our Loneliness

Psalm of the Week: Psalm 142

Day 1

FINDING HEALING IN PSALM 142

Read Psalm 142 out loud. David, the writer of this psalm, is hiding in a cave from King Saul, who is trying to kill him. Underline any verses showing that David feels alone in his troubles.

Seeing God's Heart

My precious daughter,

I see you in this dark valley. I am aware of every hidden tear shed, every shout of anger, every dream shattered. Even if you don't feel My presence, I am faithfully by your side, giving you strength and drying your tears. You are not alone.

Life has changed dramatically in ways you neither expected nor wanted, but I was not taken off guard. This is a storm I knew was coming, and I have prepared you for it in ways you do not even realize. My hand will save you and sustain you. You are not alone.

In times when you feel desperately lonely, when you think no one cares for you, remember that I am as close to you as the sunshine on your face or the breeze in your hair. I have walked each step of your path with you and sometimes carried you. Also, remember friends, women from church, family members, strangers in the store—all who have given you an encouraging word or hug. These are gifts from Me. Let those who are healthy and love you gather about you to lend support or just keep you company.

My heart aches because I know you are suffering, and I long to comfort you. Allow the pain of loneliness to create a deeper, more intimate faith–– of greater worth than gold—in Me.

I love you! I am right beside you.

Daddy

Talking to God

"My heavenly Daddy, sometimes I sense Your presence; sometimes I feel utterly alone. Help me to believe the truth that You are always with me. Open my eyes every day to see Your reminders that I am not alone."

Journaling with God

What touches me most about this letter?

Do I realize God is always with me?

How would fully realizing God's presence affect my daily life?

Psalm 142:2 says, "I pour out before him my complaint; before him I tell my trouble." What do I need to pour out to God today?

FINDING HEALING IN PSALM 142

Read Psalm 142 and observe the contrast between what men do to
David and what God does for David.

Seeking God First—Crazy Valentine

We love because he first loved us. (1 John 4:19)

I read the zaniest Valentine's Day story. Usually, I try to avoid romantic
reminders of all kinds—movies, songs, places, stories—but this one was
just too funny.

Bob Goff, an awkwardly tall man with blond afro-like hair and Levi's
with holes before holes became a fashion statement, was playing guitar at
a Young Life meeting. In walked a beautiful new volunteer he had never
seen before to help with the girls. He leaned over to his friend and whis-
pered, "That's Mrs. Goff."[3]

Ten days later, he made a Valentine's Day card out of cardboard eight
feet by four *feet* and brought it to her workplace, an advertising agency.
She refused it in embarrassment. Undaunted, he devised a new plan and
gifted her every morning with peanut butter and jelly sandwiches under
the windshield wiper of her car. He gave up his sandwich strategy after a
week with no response. She finally did decide to date him—three years
later. He concedes it might have taken less time had he initially chosen a
less stalker-like approach, but that is not the point.

His point in telling the story in his book *Love Does*, and my point in
repeating it, is to rejoice in God's pursuit of and love for us. God's desire
is relationship and intimacy, so He chases after us. *The God of the universe
pursues His wayward, imperfect children even when we are running away
from Him.* Amazing!

At the time of this writing, I am in a season that holds no romantic
love, but instead of pining for something I don't have, I try to visualize

God wooing me. After all, apart from the peanut butter and jelly sandwiches, the pursuit tactics are similar. We pursue people by giving gifts (God gave His Son), showing interest in who they are (God knows every hair on our heads), making promises for the future (God's plans for us are good), and professing our love (verses about God's love for us abound).

———

For I am convinced that neither death nor life, neither angels nor demons, neither the present nor the future, nor any powers, neither height nor depth, nor anything else in all creation, will be able to separate us from the love of God that is in Christ Jesus our Lord.
(Rom. 8:38–39)

Talking to God

"Being single again wasn't part of my plan, and You know loneliness causes an ache deep inside. Help me not to waste this alone time but take the opportunity to develop intimacy with You. Help me to be more aware of how You love and pursue me, Lord, and to grow passionately in love with You, as I know You are with me."

Journaling with God

In which circumstances do I feel most lonely?

What are some ways I combat this loneliness and experience negative results?

What are some ways I combat loneliness with positive results?

How is the image of God wooing me helpful?

FINDING HEALING IN PSALM 142

Read Psalm 142 and observe David's intense and desperate emotions.

Seeking God First—Bedbugs

Those who trust in themselves are fools, but those who walk in wisdom are kept safe. (Prov. 28:26)

A friend of mine recently discovered what looked like bedbugs and their eggs on her mattress. She immediately took action by searching on Google for advice. After she infused her mind with stories of infestations and images of bodies covered with bites, she called an exterminator and warned her roommates. Normally an avoidant, she changed her ways to confront the issue with action, knowing she wouldn't be able to sleep anyway. She stayed up until 3 a.m. spraying clothes with rubbing alcohol and vinegar and sealing them in bags, setting a trap to draw the bugs out, and then scrubbing her own body, all the time itching and jumping at every dark spot. Her roommates and others suggested she wait for the verdict from the exterminator, but she was convinced they did not see the seriousness of the situation. She refused to wait.

The verdict from the exterminator? Mostly crumbs. Possibly one dead flea and one random bug, but the rest was nothing. She had panicked, had become obsessed with obliterating something that wasn't even there. She lost money and sleep and suffered more than a little embarrassment.

Sometimes, like my friend, I react to a situation or person based on how I feel or what I have convinced myself is true. One of the strongest emotions I feel is loneliness. When I have a particularly trying day, I feel especially vulnerable and lonely and cry out in frustration. *I am so sick of doing this alone! It's all on my shoulders, and I never get any help. No one truly cares about or understands what I'm going through.* I might *feel* completely alone and have these thoughts, but that doesn't make it my reality. The truth is, God is always there, and my friends and family help whenever I ask and sometimes even when I don't ask.

Decisions based merely on feelings of loneliness can be problematic, especially in the dating world. Both men and women are vulnerable and seek to sooth the pain and begin anew to avoid being alone. However, if the relationship comes too soon or does not honor God, more loneliness and heartache will ensue.

I am not advocating that we ignore our emotions; they can be good indicators and motivators. After all, God experiences emotions—pleasure, anger, satisfaction, sadness, joy—and we were created in God's image. However, emotions can also deceive us, especially in the murky confusion of divorce, so we should examine them through the lens of God's truth and ask wise people to help us see our reality.

———

As the heavens are higher than the earth, so are my ways higher than your ways and my thoughts than your thoughts. (Isa. 55:9)

Talking to God

"Lord, forgive me for my acts that were based solely on my feelings and not on Your truth. Through Your Holy Spirit, give me discernment and wisdom in every decision, especially when I feel so emotionally distraught and confused. Develop in me the strength to control my emotions and wait patiently for Your guidance before I act."

Journaling with God

What past purely emotional decisions have I regretted?

What emotions have a stronghold on me right now?

How can I depend more on the Holy Spirit's guidance and less on my emotions of the moment?

What can I learn from David about how to deal with my emotions?

Read Psalm 142 and note where David is convinced of
God's comfort and help.

Seeking God First—Lost Keys

*When my spirit grows faint within me, it is you who
watch over my way. (Ps. 142:3)*

After helping clear chairs after the Sunday service, I couldn't locate my
keys. A thorough search of my purse, pockets, and a nearby pile of belong-
ings proved fruitless. No keys. I solicited help, and soon three or four of
us were scouring the gym. Nothing. *Where could they be? Surely somebody
would have spoken up if they had found them earlier.* Frustrated, I looked in
my purse for the umpteenth time and . . . oops. Hidden in an inner side
pocket were my keys. I had them all along.

Too often we search for something we already have. As I struggle
through the loss of my marriage, I have longed for many comforts—
security, peace, unconditional love, stability. The simple and true answer
is that I already have these comforts in Christ. I have indeed experienced
amazing love and soothing peace from God, but I wish I were more aware
of what I always have with me—God's presence.

Making decisions, cooking dinner, decompressing after a frustrating
day, or going on a bike ride are now activities I most often do alone. I long
to feel God's presence in each of these moments, but at times it eludes me.
Or at least the *feeling* of His presence does.

An acquaintance of mine, as she lay in bed at night in the midst of
very trying circumstances, physically felt God's arms around her, providing comfort and reassurance. I confess to being a bit jealous of this,
for I haven't felt His presence so tangibly, but I have sensed His presence
through the encouraging words of a friend, a sermon speaking directly to

me, the uplifting words of a song, and even sunlight splashed across my living room floor.

Increased alertness to God's presence in each moment would reduce my loneliness. That is the reality for a Christ follower, and my spirit is willing, but my flesh is weak. I forget and turn inward. In my mind and heart, however, I am convinced God is walking by my side, encouraging me, providing for me, and supporting me. I have had Him all along!

———

The LORD replied, "My Presence will go with you,
and I will give you rest." (Exod. 33:14)

Talking to God

"Lord, as I battle loneliness, I know there are practical steps I can take to have less time alone. But I ask You to help me battle this on a deeper level. Help me to believe and remember, moment by moment, that You are with me. I want to more fully experience Your presence by my side as I heal."

Journaling with God

In what ways do I struggle with believing in God's constant presence?

How can I become more cognizant of His presence on a daily basis?

What evidence of God's presence have I seen in my life today? This week?

What verse in Psalm 142 is the most comforting to me?

Finding Hope in the Stories of Two Lonely Women
(Luke 8:40–48; John 8:1–11)

Jesus lived in a time when women were seen as less valuable and significant than men, yet He treated them with respect, dignity, and love. Examine the following encounters that Jesus has with two different women. The Bible does not directly say they were lonely, but their circumstances or lifestyle would have isolated them and most likely would have produced feelings of deep loneliness and rejection. Read carefully to see how Jesus meets their situational, emotional, and spiritual needs.

According to Jewish law, a woman who was bleeding was considered ceremonially unclean, and she was not allowed to come near the temple—the center of socialization in ancient Israel. The woman in Luke 8:40–48 had been bleeding for twelve years.

Read Luke 8:40–48. Imagine you are the bleeding woman. What would you be thinking and feeling in this situation?

Why didn't Jesus just keep walking? What touches you about the *way* He heals her?

If you had the opportunity to touch Jesus's cloak for healing, what healing would you desire? Do you believe that you can receive miraculous healing?

What thoughts do you have about Jesus's parting words to the woman? What would Jesus's words to you be?

In John 8:1–11 the teachers of the law and the Pharisees brought a woman caught in adultery before Jesus to see what He would do about her punishment.

Reading this passage, what disturbs you most about the woman's situation?

What touches you about how Jesus deals with her?

What have you learned about how Jesus deals with hurting, lonely women from these two passages?

PART II

The Struggle to Face
Our New Reality

Chapter 4

Seeking God in Our Helplessness

Psalm of the Week: Psalm 23

FINDING HEALING IN PSALM 23
Read Psalm 23 out loud and observe all the things the
Shepherd does for His sheep.

Seeing God's Heart

My precious child,

I know you feel overwhelmed and helpless at times, and you wonder how you will ever manage on your own. If your mind wanders to your ever-growing to-do list, you ask yourself, "How can I get all this done? How will I ever get my life back under control?"

I have an answer for you. You can't, especially in areas where your life includes other people and their actions. You can't control your husband, who refuses to get counseling; your teenager, who chooses destructive acts; or your friend, who gives insensitive advice. You can't even control when the car will break down, the computer will freeze, or the dryer will quit. The truth is you never really had control in the first place; you just thought you had it.

This lack of control has a silver lining: it teaches you to seek Me first.

Remember that I, the Lord of heaven and earth, the maker of nations, the giver of life, am watching over you. I am an ever-present help in trouble, a constant help even in the darkest valley. I guide you, one step at a time, along the right paths and prepare the way ahead. I can give you the strength and wisdom you need to keep going.

Lay your feelings of helplessness at My feet and trust in My sovereign plan and control. Savor the sweetness of dependence on Me in ways you never have before. Watch expectantly to see how I will help you face your challenges.

Your loving God

Talking to God

"I don't like admitting that I have so little control over my life, but I feel as though I'm in a small boat with no paddles, and I'm being tossed about on the waves of life's circumstances and other people's choices. I have no power, no control. But You do, and You can give me the strength, tools, and wisdom I need to move forward. Teach me to trust and depend on You instead of grasping for control that I don't have. I praise You for Your trustworthiness!"

Journaling with God

In what ways do I feel helpless today?

In what areas have I mistakenly thought I had control in the past? In what areas do I think I have control now?

What prevents me from relying on God for help on a daily basis?

Which verse in Psalm 23 most reassures me about God's faithful help and guidance?

FINDING HEALING IN PSALM 23

Read Psalm 23 and, in verse 4, underline what the Shepherd does when the sheep are most vulnerable.

Seeking God First—Look at Me

My eyes are ever on the LORD, for only he will release my feet from the snare. (Ps. 25:15)

On a television show I watched a rescue at the scene of a serious automobile accident. The vehicle was upside down in a ditch, and firefighters had the difficult task of prying open a door to reach the woman trapped inside. Fire broke out and fuel began dripping near her head. She began to scream in panic. A paramedic dropped to the ground to get face-to-face with her, addressed her by name, and beseeched, "Look at me. I know it's scary, but we know what we're doing. We are going to extricate you safely."

In the midst of a divorce, we often feel similarly desperate and panicky. We feel trapped and helpless and see no means of escaping imminent destruction. We might even scream. We hear statements such as, Things will get better. But in fact things seem to get worse.

Picturing this rescue scene calms me as I envision God helping me. In my current difficulties, as well as the future ones I am sure to encounter, I can imagine God addressing me by name and acknowledging, not minimizing, the trial I am enduring. He knows how to extricate me safely, but I have to pay attention and trust that He is willing and able to do it. I have to stay focused on Him and not give way to panic.

I am learning to be completely honest about my fears and desperation. Many times I feel helpless, lost, and powerless. But I am best able to recognize my need for help and turn to God in those times. I imagine Him sitting next to me, lifting my head by my chin, locking His eyes on mine, and saying urgently but gently, "Becky, look at Me. I am right here. I will help you through this. It's going to be okay. Do not focus on the turmoil around you. You need to keep looking straight at Me."

God sees our tumultuous circumstances and understands our feelings of desperation. He asks us to trust Him to rescue us. He will do it in all tenderness and strength. He will lead us to a pleasant place of rest, near quiet waters.

———

Look to the LORD and his strength; seek his face always.
(1 Chron. 16:11)

Talking to God

"Lord, I don't know what my future holds, but You do. You know me, and You hold my life in Your hands. Help me to seek Your face, to trust You, and to rely on Your strength when I am afraid. You are my ever-present help in trouble."

Journaling with God

What specific circumstances have triggered feelings of helplessness in me?

How do I respond to those feelings?

How can I better seek God's face in those circumstances?

If God were to gently take my chin in His hand and look me tenderly in the eyes, what would He say to me?

FINDING HEALING IN PSALM 23

Read Psalm 23 and note all the ways the sheep are dependent on the shepherd.

Seeking God First—Redwood Trees

From him the whole body, joined and held together by every supporting ligament, grows and builds itself up in love, as each part does its work. (Eph. 4:16)

Redwood trees are amazing. Here on the Pacific coast we have at least fifty that are over three hundred and sixty feet tall and some are over two thousand years old. They are incredibly strong trees, they survive attacks by insects, and they resist fire and rot. Most amazingly, their root system only extends twelve feet deep. How does such a mammoth tree stay standing? The secret is that their root system extends sideways, up to fifty feet, and intertwines with the roots of other redwoods for support.

What a beautiful image for the body of Christ! According to God's design, we grow in strength as we develop healthy connections with each other. We can survive and even thrive in the midst of powerful tempests when connecting below the surface with other believers.

While on my journey of separation and divorce, I have benefited immensely as my sisters in Christ have supported and comforted me. One day I went to my friend's house for a writing session but could only work for about an hour. I was battling depression and shutting down—doing more staring than thinking or writing. We finally took a break while she cooked chicken and black sticky rice in her rice cooker (that spoke to her in Korean). She covered me in a blanket, put on an inspiring Christian video, and just let me rest. She didn't ask me to talk, and she didn't give advice. She simply served me, expecting nothing in return. Even as I write this, her sensitive care brings tears to my eyes.

In the dark days of my divorce, the comfort of close friends has been priceless. I am convinced my recovery would have been slower and more painful without loving friends.

Joining support groups of other women in similar circumstances provided another lifeline for me. At different times, I was in four support groups. (See appendix E for group resources.) Recently, I belonged to a Bible study with a fantastic group of single women who love the Lord and hold each other up with love, grace, and prayer. The name of our group? The Redwoods.

Therefore encourage one another and build each other up,
just as in fact you are doing. (1 Thess. 5:11)

Talking to God

"Lord Jesus, I don't like to feel needy. I have difficulty asking for and accepting support, but You have *designed* us to be relational, to receive support from others, as the redwood trees do. Thank You for that design. I see the strength and blessings that come from that support. Help me to accept love and comfort from my friends and family as gifts from You."

Journaling with God

What do I need to do today to strengthen my connections with others?

What about making these connections is difficult or risky for me?

Is it easier for me to give or receive support? Why?

I recall a time when I received or gave support, and I remember that the rewards were _____.

FINDING HEALING IN PSALM 23

Read Psalm 23 and circle the active verbs relating to movement; for example, in verse 2 circle the verb *leads*. Also circle the verbs and phrases relating to rest, such as *makes me lie down*.

Seeking God First—Push Here and Pull There

If either of them falls down, one can help the other up. But pity anyone who falls and has no one to help them up. (Eccl. 4:10)

Years ago my friend Valerie had a total hip replacement because the joint had deteriorated from rheumatoid arthritis. She was fifteen.

Instead of giving meticulous instructions about how to help Valerie get around when she left the hospital, her surgeon said to her family, "Listen to Valerie. She knows what she needs." Even at her young age, she was able to instruct her parents and siblings in how to help her carefully maneuver her way in and out of bed, the shower, the car, a chair.

Valerie still does this today. Because of multiple surgeries and ensuing scar tissue, she is no longer able to bend her knees, so whenever we go somewhere or she comes to visit at my house, she knows what she needs and she gives instructions. To negotiate the steps or sit in a chair, she tells us how many people she needs, where to stand, whether to push or pull and in what direction, and where we should grip her for the best support.

We sometimes need to be more like Valerie in communicating our needs but are often unable or reticent. We quickly dismiss questions about how to help with the ridiculous claim, "It's okay. I'm fine." Perhaps we know we need help but can't think of anything practical or tangible beyond a request for prayer.

People genuinely desire to help, and as we move toward healing, our progress will be smoother and a little less painful if we become more adept at identifying and communicating our needs. Admit that this is a season of your life in which you are needy, identify the healthy people who will support you, and then provide explicit instructions. Do you need dinner once a week? Help with the kids? Company at the doctor's office, the meeting with the attorney, the nail salon? A shoulder to cry on . . . right now?

———

When Moses' hands grew tired, they took a stone and put it under him and he sat on it. Aaron and Hur held his hands up—one on one side, one on the other—so that his hands remained steady till sunset. (Exod. 17:12)

Talking to God

"Lord, help me to recognize my neediness and be willing to ask for support. Teach me to set aside my pride, my mask of perfection, or whatever it is that stops me from asking. Give me wisdom and courage as I communicate my requests for help, both large and small, with safe people You have put in my life. I trust You for the outcome."

Journaling with God

How do I feel when I help others?

Is it difficult for me to ask for help? Why or why not?

What are two specific areas I need help in this week? Who can I ask for help? When and how will I ask for help? What do I expect their responses to be?

How is my asking and accepting help from others part of God's plan for restoring my soul?

Finding Hope in the Story of Our Shepherd (Ps. 23)

Sheep are particularly helpless creatures, dependent upon their shepherd for health and survival.[4] In Psalm 23, arguably the most well-known passage in the Bible, David describes God as his shepherd caring for him as a sheep. God is also *our* shepherd who protects and cares for us. Reflecting on God's care for David in Psalm 23 will help us receive God's loving care during this season of feeling helpless.

Read Psalm 23. To what extent do you agree with verse 1, which says, "The LORD is my shepherd, I lack nothing"?

What specifically does God do for David?

How is this kind of care evident in your life? Which verse is the most encouraging to you and why?

How does the concept of God as your shepherd reassure you and help you avoid feelings of helplessness?

Verse 3 says, "He refreshes my soul." What does that mean to you? In other words, what do you envision the refreshing of your soul to look like? Right now, to what extent do you believe this to be possible?

Chapter 5

Seeking God in Our Fear

Psalm of the Week: Psalm 27

Day 1

FINDING HEALING IN PSALM 27

Psalm 27 is another psalm written by David while King Saul and his army pursued him to kill him. Read Psalm 27 and underline the circumstances that could cause David to fear.

Seeing God's Heart

My beloved,

I know you are afraid of the future, the unknown road ahead. You don't know what's around the next dangerous curve, over the next steep hill, or even at the final destination, and this is terrifying for you. Worries about your children, finances, and health only top the long list of concerns over which you feel you have no control. These issues would be difficult to handle even if you were emotionally strong, so I understand why you are struggling.

I understand when you feel paralyzed, alone, and forgotten. I understand when you wake early in the morning, determined to conquer your fear, only to go to bed at night lost in despair. I understand, but I don't want you to stay stuck there.

You might remember My promise of prosperous plans for you, plans for a hope and a future. Though your circumstances have changed in ways that seem far from good and prosperous, My promise is still true. You do not yet comprehend the paths I have cleared, the purposes I have ordained, and the blessings I have orchestrated for you.

As we embark on this new phase of your life, don't fear what looks like a long, dark road ahead. Instead, rest in My perfect love that casts out fear. Recognize Me as your stronghold, your shelter, your salvation. Remember, I know you completely. I always want what is best for you. And I love you unconditionally—like no human can.

Our journey together, while not trouble free, will be sacred and full of mystery. You will often not know the end destination, and I may not guide you to the most direct route, but I promise it will be the best route for you. The longer we travel together, the more you will be able to release your anxieties to Me and let Me do the driving, confident of My goodness.

Will you trust Me?

Your loving Father

Talking to God

"Lord God, forgive me. Sometimes when I feel swallowed up by fear and anxiety, I just want to pull over to the side of the road and stop. I want to quit, to hide, to avoid dealing with life, especially when it involves change and taking risks. Other times, I do the opposite. In a feeble attempt to gain control, I charge far down the highway before I realize I've made a wrong turn. Help me to seek You in my fear by releasing my anxieties to You and trusting that You will keep me going in the right direction and help me overcome any obstacles along the way."

Journaling with God

What do I most fear today and why?

What is one practical thing and one spiritual thing I can do about that fear?

How does understanding God's perfect love for me help me deal with my fear and trust God more?

How would confidence in seeing "the goodness of the LORD in the land of the living" (Ps. 27:13) affect my fear?

FINDING HEALING IN PSALM 27

Read Psalm 27 and note why the psalmist does not have fear.

Seeking God First—Loosen Your Grip

I cling to you; your right hand upholds me. (Ps. 63:8)

In his book *Where Is God When It Hurts?* Philip Yancey describes Dr. Paul Brand's work with patients afflicted with leprosy. Leprosy, very simply put, is caused by bacteria that destroy the body's ability to feel pain by attacking the skin and nerves.

A lack of pain may not seem to an uninitiated bystander to be problematic; it may even sound appealing. But without pain, we will engage in activities that damage our bodies. Pain is a message sent to the brain that says, "Stop!" One of Brand's patients, Hector, showed signs of infection in his hand, between his thumb and forefinger. Since the infection did not cause any pain, Hector was unaware which activity was causing the damage. After much questioning, the doctors determined that it was mopping the canteen every day. Because Hector was unable to sense pressure, he gripped the mop handle too tightly, each time inflicting more harm to his already injured tissues.[5]

Similarly, I can cause emotional damage if I hold tightly to someone or something that is already lost. If I do not let go of those things I no longer have—the one I thought was my life partner, my extended family, united family holidays, my house, personal security—I will cause myself further pain and damage. I have to let go of these elements of my life—at least as I had once imagined them. It's scary to let go, but if I don't release them, I won't heal.

I know now that if I try to hold on to what I had before, I will miss the new dreams and blessings God has for me. As I have let parts of my old life go, I have experienced many new blessings. I have grown closer to and feel cared for by my earthly father for the first time in my life as he has helped me through my separation and divorce. My nephew and his wife, now my only extended family members in the area, have given me a standing invitation to their home for any occasion. I have met many wonderful, godly single women who support and challenge me, and most important of all, I have grown closer to the Lord.

_____

I remain confident of this: I will see the goodness of the LORD in the land of the living. Wait for the LORD; be strong and take heart and wait for the LORD. (Ps. 27:13–14)

Talking to God

"Lord, help me to hold all that is in my life loosely and be open to the changes You have planned for me. Reveal to me what I am gripping too tightly. Teach me to let go, wait patiently, and cling to You only."

Journaling with God

What have I been clutching too tightly?

In what areas of my future is it difficult for me to let go and trust God? Why is this difficult?

How can I more consistently implement letting go of earthly things and clinging to God?

To what extent is Psalm 27:1 true in my life?

What new dreams and blessings has God already supplied?

FINDING HEALING IN PSALM 27

Read Psalm 27 out loud and note where David, despite his
circumstances, feels confident in God's help.

Seeking God First—Who's Driving?

*Have I not commanded you? Be strong and courageous. Do not be
afraid; do not be discouraged, for the LORD your God will be with
you wherever you go. (Josh. 1:9)*

The road was dark, winding, and so heavily blanketed with fog I couldn't
see the cliff's edge on my right. I didn't even know it was there until my
dear friend April, who was driving, casually declared, "You wouldn't like
it if you could see what's out there." Thanks, April. Actually, this bit of
information didn't bother me; I remained relaxed, trusting her skilled
driving because she knew the road and knew her Dodge Ram truck,
which I've nicknamed *The Beast*.

Riding with my teenage daughter when she was first learning to drive
was a completely different experience. On high alert, I couldn't stop taking in my breath sharply, gripping the door handle with white knuckles,
and forcefully pressing an imaginary brake pedal—all of which added to
her anxiety. I felt out of control and feared the worst.

In the separation and divorce process, I sometimes felt a sinking feeling
of imminent doom in the pit of my stomach. During those times, my
heart rate would elevate, panic would rise in my throat, and I'd think, *I
can't do this. I'm going to fall apart. The worst is going to happen.* The funny
thing is that these attacks wouldn't always emerge in serious situations,
such as a court appearance or a counseling session. Sometimes a little
inconvenience, such as a red light or lost sunglasses, would trigger my
panic response and send me over the edge.

Fear is a healthy emotion when we need to flee or fight in harmful situations. However, there is a third response to fear, freezing, and freezing usually produces less beneficial results because nothing is done to deal with the harmful situation. This has been my typical response. Even after the initial stun wears off, I remain frozen in place. I don't do anything, expecting the problem to fade away. I ignore the issue, hoping it will get fixed on its own. I maintain the status quo, thinking I won't have to take any risks, change, or be the recipient of somebody's anger. What happens when a deer freezes in the headlights? Nothing good.

I have tried to keep moving. I take one small step to deal with what's worrying me. I call a friend, exercise, go to a movie, clean—okay, I admit, that last response is rare. My most effective response to fear, however, is to remember who is in the driver's seat. God is trustworthy and powerful, and He enables me to unfreeze and move forward, one step at a time, leaving fear on the side of the road.

———

Do not be terrified by them, for the LORD your God, who is among
you, is a great and awesome God. (Deut. 7:21)

Talking to God

"Lord, there are so many things I fear—being alone, the unknown, the finances—but You will take care of all those things. Increase my trust and give me the strength to look past my fear to You."

Journaling with God

What do I currently fear the most?

FEAR is an acronym for "false evidence appearing real." Are there things about my fears that are unrealistic? In other words, what about my forecast of the future revolves around false evidence?

How does envisioning God in the driver's seat help me deal with my fear?

FINDING HEALING IN PSALM 27

Read Psalm 27 and underline the passages in which David makes requests of God.

Seeking God First—New Year's Dance

For the Spirit God gave us does not make us timid, but gives us power, love and self-discipline. (2 Tim. 1:7)

I am not a dancer. I am introverted, reserved, currently suspicious of most men, and not interested in dating, and as the saying goes, I have two left feet. So why was I going to my church's singles group's New Year's dance?

As much of the day was being swallowed up in the physical rituals of beautification—getting a French manicure, attempting a do-it-yourself pedicure, tweezing, shaving, styling, sighing—I asked myself that question . . . repeatedly. The answer was clear: I had been coerced.

My dear friend April, a highly sought and enthusiastic dance partner at these events, forced me go. Maybe that word is a bit strong, but she has this annoying habit of asking probing questions and challenging me to do things that make me, at minimum, squirm in discomfort. So I put on my fancy navy blue dress with a plunging neckline, pinned up the too-plunging neckline, put a scarf over the stare-at-my-cleavage plunging neckline, and squirmed out the door, fearing the long night ahead.

I didn't even last until midnight, not because I was having a terrible time but because I didn't need to be there anymore. I had fulfilled my promise to go, I had faced my fear and discomfort, and then I chose to go home because I was tired and just not that interested. Next year when April invites me to go with her, and I know she will, I will probably decline, opting for game night instead. My refusal, however, will not be based on fear of the unknown or a desire to avoid pain and discomfort; it will be based on who I am and what I want to do or not do.

As I create a new life as a divorced woman, at minimum, I squirm. This new life is painful, disorienting, awkward, and frustrating. But it doesn't have to stay that way. I can allow myself to feel the discomfort but then find freedom in choice, and rest in God's miraculous design of who I am and who He has called me to be.

Ironically, although I still have two left feet, I am no longer opposed to dancing . . . with a group of friends . . . when I'm in a good mood. What I once feared, I now enjoy on occasion.

––––

Fear of man will prove to be a snare, but whoever trusts in the LORD is kept safe. (Prov. 29:25)

Talking to God

"Thank You, Jesus, for teaching me that facing my fear brings freedom. Help me to stride boldly into the unknown, assured of Your presence, support, and guidance. Thank You for being the dance partner who never leaves my side. And thank You for friends who encourage me to step out of my comfort zone."

Journaling with God

In the last month what are three things I have avoided doing out of fear?

Under what conditions am I better able to face my fears?

This week, what is one thing I can do to face my fears?

How can I better seek God in the midst of my fearful circumstances?

Finding Hope in Nehemiah's Story (Neh. 4; 6:15–16)

The Babylonians had destroyed the walled city of Jerusalem and exiled the Jews to other countries one hundred and fifty years prior to the time of Nehemiah. A remnant of the exiled Jews had returned to Jerusalem, but the city remained in ruins.

While still in exile, Nehemiah, the king's cupbearer, learns that Jerusalem is still in ruins, and he is grief-stricken. In performing the duty of tasting the king's wine to ensure that it had not been poisoned, he had gained the trust and favor of King Artaxerxes of Babylon. So his request is granted when, after three months of prayer, he asks the king for a leave of absence to go and repair the wall surrounding the city. However, as we see in chapters 4 through 6, Nehemiah and the Jewish people face opposition to their work.

This restoration of the city wall for strength and protection is akin to the rebuilding of our lives for our own well-being and God's glory. As we face the monumental task of repairing and restoring our lives, we will encounter both internal and external opposition, just as Nehemiah did.

Which part of your life seems the most difficult to repair right now?

Read Nehemiah 4:1–6, which relates the mocking criticisms of foreign officials who feared the strengthening of Israel. What doubts about rebuilding might have been raised by these comments? In what ways do you relate to doubts about rebuilding your life?

In what ways do you relate to the Jews' response to increased opposition in 4:7–12?

What do you appreciate about Nehemiah's practical and spiritual response to the opposition in 4:13–23? How can you apply this to your own situation?

What encourages you about Nehemiah 6:15–16?

Chapter 6

Seeking God in Our Guilt

Psalm of the Week: Psalm 51

Day 1

FINDING HEALING IN PSALM 51

Psalm 51 was written by David after he had committed adultery.
Read Psalm 51 and underline all the requests David makes of God
regarding his sin.

Seeing God's Heart

My precious daughter,

Why are you hiding from Me? Yes, you have done some wrong things
and there will be natural consequences for those sins, but running from
Me only hurts us more. I desire to draw you back into My arms to heal
you, not scold you.

I'm not shocked by your actions or thoughts. I'm not even disappointed
or displeased, but I am grieved. I'm saddened because our relationship has
been damaged; I'm still here, but you have moved far away from Me.
You've been avoiding Me and ignoring Me.

Remember, I am your good and perfect heavenly Father. I desire to
give you the gifts of forgiveness, peace, and joy. Even an earthly father
knows not to give a stone when his daughter asks for bread. Through My

Son, Jesus, I have given you the best gift a father can give: freedom from any condemning thoughts, words, or actions. I have cleansed you from your sin; you are washed whiter than snow.

You can't earn forgiveness by feeling bad. Just ask for it, accept it, and stop beating yourself up. It is finished. You can stop dwelling on the past and move forward.

Remember that I know you even better than you know yourself. I know the pain that has prompted you to stray from Me and the circumstances that brought the temptation. I know your regrets from the past, your judgmental thoughts about yourself and others, and your unhealthy choices to numb your pain.

I also know the accuser, who plants condemning thoughts in your mind. He is the Father of Lies, who wants to keep you mired in misery and guilt. He wants you trapped in repeated thoughts of self-condemnation, draining you of the abundant life of freedom and joy I have for you.

Yes, you will have to deal with some consequences of your actions, but let Me help you. Allow Me to bring good from the situation, because I love you, because I delight in drawing you close to Me. Let Me restore to you the joy of My salvation.

In all of your imperfections, flaws, and brokenness, I have chosen you. Let My Spirit, like a strong wind, clear your mind and heart of guilt, freeing you to become all that I have created you to be. Draw near to Me, and let's walk this journey of abundant life together.

Your merciful God

Talking to God

"Father God, thank You for Your mercy and forgiveness. I don't deserve it and could never earn it, but You freely give it to me because You want a relationship with me. That amazes me! Help me to believe each moment of the day that I am pure and free of sin because of the sacrifice of Your Son."

Journaling with God

Which part of the letter affected me the most and why?

What sins do I repeatedly feel guilty about?

How do I think God views me when I sin?

Do I believe that God cleanses me of my sin and makes me *whiter than snow* (Ps. 51:7)?

FINDING HEALING IN PSALM 51

Read Psalm 51 out loud and note aspects of God's character that make forgiveness possible.

Seeking God First—Banana Bread

Therefore, there is now no condemnation for those who are in Christ Jesus, because through Christ Jesus the law of the Spirit who gives life has set you free from the law of sin and death. (Rom. 8:1–2)

I have to brag—I make delicious banana bread. Granted, as far as culinary sophistication goes, the recipe is extremely simple and calls for common ingredients, but somehow I receive showers of compliments . . . usually.

Occasionally, I alter the ingredients, either by design or by accident. By design, I sometimes add semisweet chocolate chips, thinking any baked goods deserve a chocolate complement, and I receive mixed reactions, depending on the intensity of the eater's sweet tooth.

Twice, I have altered the recipe by accident. One time, in my haste and a multitasking frenzy, I forgot to add flour, resulting in banana bread that resembled the shape—and maybe even the taste—of a brick. To avoid wasting the food and effort, I tried to suffer through it by lathering it with a thick coat of butter. That was just a waste of butter. I eventually gave up, offered some to the dog—who will eat anything—and threw the rest away.

The second accidental alteration was much worse. Instead of a teaspoon, I added a tablespoon of salt. One bite of this culinary disaster doomed it to the garbage can. There was no escaping the overpowering saltiness; no amount of butter, sugar, or even melted chocolate chips could have masked my mistake.

As that tablespoon of salt saturated the batter and spoiled the banana bread, so guilt can pervade our minds and hearts until our lives seem unpalatable, irreparable, and worthless.

Simply put, guilt—false guilt, worldly sorrow, and shame—is the negative feeling we have after we have done something wrong, and the list of misdeeds, whether in our heads or in reality, is endless. This type of guilt nags, accuses, condemns, and debilitates, enveloping us in a thick fog of despair from which we can see no escape. From there we isolate ourselves from others and avoid God. We consider ourselves hopeless. This pleases Satan.

In contrast, conviction from the Holy Spirit, or godly sorrow, convinces us that a specific action was wrong. Conviction exposes and illuminates our sin. Holy sorrow grieves us for a time and motivates us toward good change. It leads us away from sin's destructive influence while drawing us toward God and His restorative grace. When we confess, we are assured of forgiveness, love, and reconciliation. We are cleansed and purified, as white as snow in God's eyes. This pleases God.

Once divorced, we find ourselves no longer able to engage in sex under the confines of our marriage, which creates a difficult situation. Sex is a powerful, natural, God-created act that promotes physical, emotional, and spiritual intimacy. However, engaging in sex in an unhealthy manner or outside of marriage can be very destructive. I'm sure we've all experienced the harmful effects of inappropriate sexual behavior; I don't know anybody who hasn't committed a sexual sin, whether in thought or deed. As we deal with the repercussions, it's important to discern whether we are experiencing false guilt from Satan or true conviction from the Holy Spirit. The following table displays the differences in our thoughts, depending on whether we're feeling false guilt or conviction regarding sexual sin.

As we deal with sin in our lives (past, present, and future), let us listen to the conviction of the Holy Spirit. After all, who wants to eat salty banana bread?

False Guilt from Satan (Worldly Sorrow)	Conviction from the Holy Spirit (Godly Sorrow)
I shouldn't do those filthy acts. What's wrong with me? Why do I keep doing this over and over again?	Those acts cheapen God's gift to me, and it will be best for me to stop. I am God's precious daughter, whom He loves, and He has a better life for me.
Why did I sleep with him? I have no self-control and I never will have any!	It was a sin and not in God the Father's will for me to sleep with him. I can see how this act that I thought would relieve my pain actually hurt me. I need to stay close to God for comfort and restoration.
I think too much about sex. I'm not a very good Christian, and God is going to reject me because of my thought life.	Healthy sexual desires are natural and do not separate me from God. I certainly should strive to honor God with my thought life, but I am confident that nothing separates me from the love of God.

Godly sorrow brings repentance that leads to salvation and leaves no regret, but worldly sorrow brings death. (2 Cor. 7:10)

Talking to God

"Heavenly Father, I admit I am confused. Do I feel false guilt or conviction? Sometimes I am not sure. Help me to discern the difference and reject any thoughts that condemn me and separate me from You. Teach me to listen better to the Holy Spirit to more clearly see behaviors I need to change but also to realize the grace, forgiveness, and strength You provide to conquer those behaviors. Most of all, thank You that I am righteous and holy in Your sight, no longer condemned."

Journaling with God

Why is it difficult for me to discern the difference between false guilt or worldly sorrow, and conviction or godly sorrow?

What do I feel bad about or responsible for in my divorce?

As I think about these things, do I feel false guilt (that I am bad) or conviction (drawn by God's love into a desire to change)?

How are my thoughts and actions regarding myself and my relationship with God affected when I have conviction from the Holy Spirit?

How do I relate to David's prayer in Psalm 51?

FINDING HEALING IN PSALM 51

Read Psalm 51 and note the places where David is hoping for
God's forgiveness.

Seeking God First—What Do You Like About Yourself?

*To claim the truths about who we are, where we come from, what
we believe, and the very imperfect nature of our lives, we have to be
willing to give ourselves a break and appreciate the beauty of our
cracks or imperfections.* —Brené Brown, Daring Greatly

I was crying, but I didn't know why. After hearing a message at a Christian
conference during my freshman year in college, I asked to speak to one of
the counselors. At one point the counselor asked me what I liked about
myself. This question surprised me, but I tried to think of something. "I'm
thoughtful of others," I said.

Actually, I'm not telling the whole truth. My complete answer was:
"I'm thoughtful of others . . . but I don't follow through enough on my
good intentions." Wow. For the first time in my life, I realized how critical
of myself I was. There was a *but* after every positive statement. My actions
were never enough. I was never enough. These thoughts and feelings of
self-condemnation came flooding back when my marriage failed. More of
them cropped up when I was writing this book, revealing a tendency to
live condemned.

The expressions "weighed down by guilt" and "burdened by guilt"
aptly describe the paralyzing heaviness of guilt. We know perfection is
impossible, but we beat ourselves up when we don't attain it. We know
mistakes are inevitable, but we condemn ourselves when we make them,
especially as we face the end of a marriage.

Hoping we will collapse in despair, Satan accuses us and fills our minds
with guilt and shaming thoughts:

I didn't do enough to save my marriage. I gave up too soon.
I didn't love him enough to get him to stay with me.
I wasn't a good enough Christian, and I'm still not.
I didn't pray enough for my marriage.
My kids are now damaged, and it's my fault.
My kids are acting out, and it's all because of my divorce.
I'm a terrible mother.
I wasn't a good wife.
My relief that it's over proves that I didn't care enough about the sanctity
  of marriage.
My sexual sin proves that I'm a weak Christian.
It's my fault, because I had an affair.
It's my fault that he had an affair.
I'm a bad example to non-Christians.
I'm not smart enough. I'm not pretty enough. I'm not loving enough.

These accusations could go on and on and on, and they do if we let them. Our challenge is to respond to conviction from the Holy Spirit and reject guilt from Satan (see the previous day's devotion). We need to accept the reality of God's forgiveness and then identify and reject Satan's lies. This involves the retraining of our minds. Brené Brown acknowledged the need to retrain our minds when she said that "a strong belief in our own worthiness doesn't just happen—it's cultivated."[6]

The absolutely fantastic news is that God never expected perfection. Bathed in His love and grace through Christ, we stand before Him, perfectly loved, completely pure, and wonderfully treasured. We can't earn His unconditional love; we already have it.

My friend Mary battles Satan's lies with Scripture. As soon as an accusation pops into her mind, she speaks God's truth out loud—there's something uniquely powerful about *hearing* truth. One of her favorite verses is 1 Peter 2:9, which states: "But you are a chosen people, a royal priesthood, a holy nation, God's special possession, that you may declare the praises of him who called you out of darkness into his wonderful light."

I am chosen. I am holy. The more I dwell on these truths, the more I renew my mind and accept and appreciate all that God has created me to be. Then I can better love Him, others, and even myself for His glory.

———

Do not conform to the pattern of this world, but be transformed
by the renewing of your mind. Then you will be able to test and
approve what God's will is—his good, pleasing and perfect will.
(Rom. 12:2)

Talking to God

"Lord God, I need help renewing my mind. Some lies seem so deeply ingrained in my thinking, that I have difficulty recognizing them as lies, let alone removing them. Help me to see myself, my circumstances, my children, my ex-husband as You see them. Give me clarity and understanding as I seek You."

Journaling with God

Which of the above accusations most resonate with me? What further accusations would I add? (It's important to name the lies.)

When I am accused, what's my typical response?

How well do I accept the truths of being chosen, holy, and fully loved by God?

What verses, whether from Psalm 51, these devotionals, or my own Bible reading, can I commit to memory in order to train my mind to focus on God's truths?

FINDING HEALING IN PSALM 51
Read Psalm 51 and note the benefits of a guilt-free heart in verses 7 through 15.

Seeking God First—Clean Your Room!

Have mercy on me, O God, according to your unfailing love;
according to your great compassion blot out my transgressions.
(Ps. 51:1)

My mom and sister are very clean and organized people—something went wrong with me. If I have company coming, I desperately scrub and declutter for two frantic hours before they arrive, praying against early birds and throwing stacks of mail, laundry, and books on my bed at the last minute. Only my closest friends have surprise drop-by privileges because I am confident they will still like me even after they see the naturally messy state of my house.

I developed this habit as early as age four or five. One day my mother deemed my room a disaster, and she refused to release me from its four walls until I had cleaned everything up. Toys, games, dolls, stuffed animals, and books did blanket every horizontal surface, especially the floor, but to be fair, nothing flowed into other areas of the house. Being confined to my room wasn't such a bad punishment—I continued playing in the mess.

After receiving a second and louder admonishment an hour later, I decided I had better get to work. Then a brilliant thought struck me. I could just shove everything in the closet! My closet was currently clean—she had no reason to inspect it, and I would be freed without doing the work I dreaded. I quickly scooped, swept, kicked, and shoved every toy within sight into the closet, closed the door, brushed my hands together in self-congratulations and confidence, and ran to get my mother. Perhaps my speed was my undoing. She soon discovered the closet clutter and scolded me, more for my deception than my mess.

Now the job was even harder. Everything was mixed together in one big pile, Barbie shoes in books, plastic animals in my shoes, and Candy Land cards everywhere. This would take a ridiculously long time, and I would miss my beloved *Lassie* show on TV (or was it *Flipper?*). So I shoved everything under the bed and waited.

Needless to say, the currently popular definition of insanity—doing the same action yet expecting different results—applied here, but I was only five—and I did strategically wait the second time. Soon, my mom eyed me with suspicion, glanced under the bed, gave me that you-know-better look moms have perfected, and left the room without a word. Feeling bad about trying to trick her again, I sighed with resignation and began cleaning in earnest. When I eventually passed inspection, I was relieved, content, and even proud of myself for finally doing it right. My mom released me from my temporary prison with a tight hug and said, "I love you," but I suspected she loved me even when my room was a mess.

This could be a story about repentance. Repentance is more than feeling sorry for what we have done, and certainly more than feeling sorry that we got caught. Repentance involves changing directions. We sense the Holy Spirit's conviction that our thoughts, actions, inactions, or attitudes are wrong; we ask forgiveness in a spirit of sincere remorse; and then we change directions. We turn away from the sin and toward God. We look to God's grace and power to free us from our sin. *Repent* is a word of invitation, not condemnation, a call to be alive in the riches of His mercy and grace instead of burdened and trapped by guilt.

We may have a heightened sense of the need to repent during this season of our lives. No matter what our spouse has done, we have our own sin to face in our marriage, in our divorce, and in our new single life. Instead of closing our eyes to it, instead of repeating it, we need to change directions and turn to God. Will we sin in the same way again? Perhaps. Will we struggle in these same areas in the future? Probably. Will God continue to forgive and want a relationship with us? Definitely.

――――

Repent, then, and turn to God, so that your sins may be wiped out,
that times of refreshing may come from the Lord. (Acts 3:19)

Talking to God

"Lord, I can think of so many sins I need to repent of that I feel over-whelmed. Anger and resentment keep surfacing in my life in unhealthy ways. Help me to not attempt to remove this by my own willpower but to turn to You in repentance. Forgive me and help me to change."

Journaling with God

What sin is weighing heavily on my heart and mind right now?

Do I believe God is prompting me to take action regarding this sin? Should I talk with a trusted friend or therapist regarding this action?

Regarding changing directions, is there a temptation I need to flee from? What safe person, who will hold me accountable, can I share this with?

Finding Hope in the Story of the Woman at the Well
(John 4:1–30, 39–42)

Jewish custom dictated that good Jewish men did not have contact with Samaritans (half Jewish people), as they were considered unclean. Talking with a woman alone would also have been inappropriate. Yet Jesus does both in this passage. As you read the passage, notice how Jesus deals with the Samaritan woman's sin and consider her response.

What do you learn about the woman in John 4:1–30? In what ways can you relate to her?

What do you learn about how Jesus views her past by how He interacts with her?

What can you assume about her new life, her new identity, from John 4:39–42?

What lesson can you learn from this passage about dealing with past guilt?

Chapter 7

Seeking God to Forgive

Psalm of the Week: Psalm 73

Day 1

FINDING HEALING IN PSALM 73

As we struggle to forgive, we may see ourselves as pure and those who have wronged us as ungodly and selfish. We certainly have our own sins of which to repent, but that is not the focus of this chapter. The goal of this chapter is to offer insight on how to forgive those who have wronged us, not to claim we are without our own sin and needing forgiveness.

In Psalm 73, the writer describes the prosperous life of the wicked but does not directly address the issue of forgiving them. However, the psalmist does wrestle with an embittered spirit, which we easily develop when we lack forgiveness in our hearts. In the psalmist's case, his bitterness comes from seeing the wicked prosper without judgment while he, a godly man, endures troubles. The psalmist demonstrates the necessary foundation for forgiveness: trusting God for vindication, for He will ultimately judge, and prioritizing drawing near to God. Read Psalm 73 out loud and observe how the writer's attitude changes from the beginning to the end of the psalm.

Seeing God's Heart

My cherished daughter,

I know you've been hurt. What happened wasn't right or fair. You may think the person or persons who harmed you don't deserve forgiveness, especially if they haven't apologized. You might not even want to consider forgiveness because you have a righteous anger. You have been wronged. They owe you. They should be punished.

You may even envy them, especially your ex-husband, imagining he is prosperous, happy, and not struggling. Perhaps you are even angry at Me, thinking I have blessed his life but not yours despite your faithfulness.

I understand all these thoughts and emotions, but remember that I will deal with those who are far from me. That is not your concern. Instead, I urge you to do something that sounds difficult, maybe even unreasonable. I want you to forgive the people who have done you harm.

Don't panic. I'm not asking you to take the leap to complete forgiveness right now. Ask Me to give you the desire to forgive and then take it one step at a time. I won't leave you alone in the process. I will be with you. With My help, you'll find forgiving others not only possible, but a necessary part of your healing process.

Be assured of My grace and patience as you struggle to forgive. Ask Me for understanding of what forgiveness is and what it is not, and be wary of conflicting or wrong advice from well-meaning people. Please understand that forgiveness does not mean condoning, ignoring, or diminishing the wrongs done to you. It does not mean you won't hurt anymore; you will still need healing. It *does* mean laying down or forgiving the debt they owe you. They can never pay it because they cannot undo what they have done, so for your own sake, let it go.

Have you been listening, dear child? Forgiveness is necessary for *your* healing. Forgiveness is for *your* sake. Forgiveness includes forgiving yourself just as I have forgiven you. My heart aches when I see you stuck in this prison of regret, anger, and bitterness, cut off from the freedom and blessings I have for you.

Climbing the mountain of forgiveness is a tough, exhausting climb but worth the view from the top. By forgiving others and yourself, you will receive freedom, peace, and an awe-inspiring new perspective. And you will be near to Me. This is the life I want for you.

Love,

  Your forgiving God

Talking to God

"Father God, I don't even want to deal with forgiving right now, but it's a relief to know forgiveness does not mean excusing the other person's behavior. It's also a relief to know it can be a process. I don't get it when people seem to forgive easily and quickly. Am I just not strong enough in my faith to do that? Help me to understand what forgiveness really means and create in my heart the desire to forgive just as You have forgiven me."

Journaling with God

Which sentence in the letter strikes me as most meaningful and why?

Which thought about sinners from Psalm 73 can I most relate to?

What is my understanding of the meaning of forgiveness? What are the benefits?

What do I think God expects of me regarding forgiveness?

FINDING HEALING IN PSALM 73

Read Psalm 73 and note what new understanding about God helps the writer overcome his strong feelings about the wicked.

Seeking God First—Autopilot

Be kind and compassionate to one another, forgiving each other, just as in Christ God forgave you. (Eph. 4:32)

One night my plan was to drive straight from work to the golf range, which is on my way home. I missed the exit, as I have done several times in the past. My brain is trained to drive home, and I was functioning on autopilot, letting my mind wander to thoughts of the day, and I didn't even notice the exit. Have you ever driven home and not remembered how you got there?

Experts say these habits are lodged deep within our brains, so we perform our routines without much conscious effort or even awareness. These routines can be good or bad, however, and during the separation and divorce season of my life, I had developed a routine of reacting in anger.

It seemed my brain automatically drove toward angrily embracing a victim mentality, and I never noticed opportunities to exit. When overwhelmed with the devastation to my family, I erupted in anger at the slightest provocation. I yelled. I screamed. I blamed. I withdrew in silence. Not all the time, of course, but I once overheard my younger daughter ask her sister, "What kind of mood is Mom in today?" That sounded like a question from a child with an alcoholic parent, not a mild-mannered, even-keeled, gentle soul like me. What had I become? I had slipped and lost my foothold, as the author of Psalm 73 almost did.

"How do I deal with all of this anger?" I asked my therapist. She responded with the F word. Not the four-letter one. The seven-letter one:

f-o-r-g-i-v-e. My therapist claimed that if I could forgive, the anger would dissipate. I had to sever the link between anger and my new life. I had to forgive. But how? I confess this area has been and remains a challenge for me, and I have no easy answers.

One effective strategy for me in the journey of forgiveness has been to take captive or redirect my thoughts to good things (2 Cor. 10:5). If I linger in the dark place where my anger lures me, I will replay the painful events over and over, becoming trapped in a life of depression, powerlessness, and regret. In contrast, if I let go and trust God to deal with others justly according to their actions, I free myself to forgive and move on.

We can have righteous, appropriate anger that spurs us to act, but if we remain embroiled in our anger for too long, forgiveness becomes harder and harder, and we imprison ourselves in a life without joy. The choice is ours. Are we ready to stop fueling the fire of anger and begin the hard work of forgiveness? Do we want to keep driving down the highway on autopilot or take the forgiveness exit?

———

My flesh and my heart may fail, but God is the strength of my heart and my portion forever. (Ps. 73:26)

Talking to God

"God, I can't do this on my own. I need Your Holy Spirit to work on my mind and heart to free me from my anger over the wrongs done to me. Help me also to more fully understand Your mercy and grace toward me in regard to my own sin. Thank You ahead of time for empowering me to step into this process of beginning to forgive."

Journaling with God

Have I forgiven my (ex-)husband? What about others (family and friends) who have hurt me?

What has helped me to forgive them? What has hampered my attempts to forgive them?

According to Psalm 73, what happens when we think others are unfairly blessed and we are unfairly punished (vv. 21–22)? Have I seen this in my life?

How can I rely on God's strength to help me forgive?

FINDING HEALING IN PSALM 73

Read Psalm 73 and underline verses that describe the writer's relationship with God.

Seeking God First—A Sweet Fragrance

Though you have made me see troubles, many and bitter, you will restore my life again; from the depths of the earth you will again bring me up. (Ps. 71:20)

When entering our local shopping mecca, the Galleria Mall, I was welcomed by what was meant to be an enticing fresh fragrance of carnations. I gagged.

The smell assaulted my sinuses, producing nausea in my stomach and heaviness in my chest. At first I didn't understand why I was suddenly tense, angry, and sad, but then I realized that the fragrance was a trigger. It promptly took me back to a time when my ex-husband and I would come to this mall to walk in the heat of summer. The floral smell reminded me of what I had lost. These triggers don't help when I am trying to forgive.

Most people don't have a distinct moment in which they completely surrendered all their anger toward another and experienced sweet release from the emotional and spiritual prison of bitterness. Of course there are exceptions when God's love and forgiveness miraculously and suddenly flow through us, such as in the well-known story from *The Hiding Place* of Corrie ten Boom forgiving an SS guard.

After World War II, Corrie preached throughout Europe, including in Germany, about God's forgiveness of our sins and the need to extend that forgiveness to others. Corrie had been arrested for hiding Jews in Holland and had spent time in Ravensbrück concentration camp, where her sister had died. One night in 1947, a man approached her after her sermon. She recognized him as one of the brutal SS guards from Ravensbrück. He had become a Christian and had accepted God's forgiveness, but wanted hers as well, and extended his hand to receive it. Corrie struggled:

> His hand was thrust to shake mine. And I, who had preached so often to the people in Bloemendaal the need to forgive, kept my hand at my side.
>
> Even as the angry, vengeful thoughts boiled through me, I saw the sin of them. Jesus Christ had died for this man; was I going to ask for more? *Lord Jesus,* I prayed, *forgive me and help me to forgive him.*
>
> I tried to smile. I struggled to raise my hand. I could not. I felt nothing, not the slightest spark of warmth or charity. And so again I breathed a silent prayer. *Jesus, I cannot forgive him. Give me Your forgiveness.*
>
> As I took his hand the most incredible thing happened. From my shoulder along my arm and through my hand, a current seemed to pass from me to him, while into my heart sprang a love for this stranger that almost overwhelmed me.
>
> And so I discovered that it is not on our forgiveness any more than on our goodness that the world's healing hinges, but on His. When He tells us to love our enemies, He gives, along with the command, the love itself.[7]

For me, forgiveness has been a process—sometimes forward and sometimes backward—and I accept that it might not happen as suddenly and miraculously as it did with Corrie. In *Forgiveness: Finding Peace Through Letting Go,* Adam Hamilton describes forgiveness as a journey, a *process* in which we "chip away slowly at these giant stones and pray that God will help us let go of the pain."[8] Forgiving my ex-husband has been a complex, recurring process. I can't cross it off a to-do list today and expect to be done with it forever. I have to revisit forgiveness, reexamine my heart, ask God for His love, and repeatedly let go, especially when my emotions get triggered.

Triggers can bring pain and anger to the surface with lightning speed and threaten to undo the hard work of forgiveness. Some triggers, such as certain dates, places, or holidays, are obvious, but others are more obscure and unexpected, like the smell in the mall. Identifying, avoiding, and combatting our triggers help us steer clear of blindsiding pain so we can move forward on the journey of healing and forgiveness.

Bear with each other and forgive one another if any of you has a grievance against someone. Forgive as the Lord forgave you.
(Col. 3:13)

Talking to God

"Father, I struggle with reminders of my hurt. I want to give up my anger, and I want to forgive—usually—but I don't think I can on my own. Give me the desire, understanding, and strength to forgive even when everyday events trigger my pain."

Journaling with God

What are my top five triggers?

What are my reactions to these triggers?

In what ways can I deal with these triggers so that I do not end up revisiting my anger?

How does my relationship with God help me deal with my triggers, especially if the triggers are people?

FINDING HEALING IN PSALM 73

Read Psalm 73 and focus on the last verse. Think about why the writer ended the psalm in this way.

Seeking God First—Forget Me Not

[Love] does not dishonor others, it is not self-seeking, it is not easily angered, it keeps no record of wrongs. (1 Cor. 13:5)

Today I tried unsuccessfully to open my seldom-used Gmail account on a new device. I tried all my usual passwords, playing with capital letters and number variations to no avail. Not wanting to change my password, I switched to my phone where it simply opens my account, no thinking or remembering required.

I sometimes wish offenses against me were similar to passwords—easy to forget and sometimes impossible to remember. If I could completely forget certain things, a sort of selective amnesia, forgiveness would be easier. I would no longer feel the sting of the hurtful words, the heartbreak of rejection, or the bitterness of suffering from repeated wrongs done against me.

But simply forgetting, even if it were possible, is not forgiveness, and it might be dangerous if it were. We need to guard our hearts and remember the actions of unsafe people so we don't expose ourselves to further harm. If we get bit by a dog, we could forgive the dog, but we might not ever pet the dog again because we remember the previous hurtful result.

Forgetting is problematic for another reason. New offenses occur. In our battles over the children, finances, and the influence of new relationships, we will inevitably be hurt again, bit by the dog again even if we try to stay away.

Recently I was angry over a financial disagreement. At a time when I thought I was done with anger, it welled up inside me, producing bitterness and resentment. I started comparing my financial situation to his and insisted that it wasn't fair. I became short-tempered. A few snide comments slipped out in front of my daughter and made her feel stressed and uncomfortable, which was not my intention at all. I didn't like who I was becoming. I was letting his actions (or lack of action) control my emotions and my happiness.

I needed to let go. I needed to stop playing the victim and own my choices. That didn't mean I had to forget about the financial disagreement, but it did mean I had to take responsibility for my reaction to the situation. How I react, how I feel, and what I do with those feelings are all up to me. Rejecting a victim mentality and owning my responsibility felt incredibly empowering and freeing.

Giving up our victim status—*forgetting* our roles as victims—is crucial for forgiveness. When we forgive, we are at peace and empowered to move on. We are free to live fully, as God intended us to live.

If you, LORD, kept a record of sins, Lord, who could stand? But with you there is forgiveness, so that we can, with reverence, serve you. (Ps. 130:3–4)

Talking to God

"Father God, only You can give me the strength to release the bitterness and resentment I sometimes feel. Help me to see and experience the liberating peace You have for me as I choose to let go and draw near to You."

Journaling with God

How difficult is it for me to forgive somebody who has wronged me? Why?

Do I sometimes think of myself as a victim, and if so, how does that affect my ability to forgive?

Do I see how forgiveness can be freeing and empowering? Why or why not?

What role does God play in helping me forgive others?

Finding Hope in Joseph's Story (Gen. 45:1–15)

In today's study we will look at a man who had much to forgive. Joseph had been sold as a slave by his own brothers, forcibly taken to Egypt, falsely accused of assault by an official's wife, and thrown into prison. After two years in prison, he correctly interpreted Pharaoh's dream and predicted seven years of plenty and seven years of famine. Pharaoh (the King of Egypt) was so pleased to know the meaning of the dream that he put Joseph in charge of Egypt (Gen. 41:41).

During the famine, Joseph's brothers learn of available food in Egypt and travel there to get some to take home. They are unaware that their own brother Joseph, whom they had sold, is in charge. Joseph does not reveal his identity right away but has the youngest brother accused of stealing to test the reaction of the others (Gen. 44).

From what you know about Joseph from the summary above or your previous Bible reading, what might Joseph have in common with the author of Psalm 73?

Read about Joseph revealing his identity to his brothers in Genesis 45:1–15. What strikes you about Joseph's response to his brothers?

How do you feel about Joseph's view of God's role in the situation?

How is your forgiveness journey different from and similar to Joseph's?

What is your main takeaway from this passage about forgiveness?

PART III

The Promise of Restoration and Healing

Chapter 8

Seeking God for Hope

Psalm of the Week: Psalm 107

Day 1

FINDING HEALING IN PSALM 107
Read Psalm 107 out loud and note the key themes in the refrain that is repeated four times.

Seeing God's Heart

My treasured daughter,

True, life will never be the same, but you will not always feel the way you do today. You will heal.

You do not need to strive for healing—simply draw close to Me. Rest in Me. Rest secure in My love for you, knowing that I am the Master Healer. When wanderers cry out to Me, I lead them to straight paths; I set prisoners free, rescue rebels from their own destruction, and save those who are in distress. In your distress, remember, the power of My healing is beyond what you can fathom. It is miraculous and not based on what *you* can or cannot do.

Yes, I know healing seems agonizingly slow. Pain and anger, some of which you thought you had left behind, are so easily triggered. Sometimes you might be able to avoid the triggers, but other times they are unexpected and inescapable. And then the tears flow again. As the tears come, rest in My warm embrace, knowing you are right where I want you to be—close to Me.

Be assured that I don't expect you to always be strong, to consistently move forward with no setbacks, to recover quickly. You will make imperfect progress. Believe that I am more patient than you are during this healing journey.

My greatest desire is that you keep crying out to Me, keep seeking a relationship with Me. The pace of your growth doesn't matter. You are My cherished daughter whom I long to heal.

Your loving Daddy

Talking to God

"Heavenly Father, Thank You for the hope of healing. This hope keeps me moving forward instead of giving up in despair. Forgive me for my impatience. Please help me to take one imperfect day at a time and to believe in complete healing as I draw near to You."

Journaling with God

Which part of the letter most resonates with me?

What does it mean to me that God saves me, rescues me, delivers me, and brings me out of my distress?

What are my hopes for the next year?

How am I depending on God for healing?

FINDING HEALING IN PSALM 107
Read Psalm 107 and circle each different situation.

Seeking God First—Coffee Mugs

I will remember the deeds of the LORD; yes, I will remember your miracles of long ago. (Ps. 77:11)

As I slowly sip my coffee, savoring a few quiet moments before the rush of the day, I pause and look at the mug. It's my favorite. I like the size—a little larger than average—and the image on the side—old books in muted shades of brown and red. The books are from Thomas Jefferson's library, and his signature encircles the bottom of the mug.

I love books, bookstores, libraries, and just about anything related to books, but that is not the primary reason this is my favorite mug. This mug elicits memories of a trip with my sister and dad to Washington, DC. When we toured the Library of Congress, instead of merely peering through the second-floor window into the main room, we applied for library cards and reverently entered the room. We walked under ornate marble arches and among well-worn, sacred books, taking in the hallowed history of the room.

My library mug is not the only cup that triggers memories. Whenever I take a trip I buy a coffee mug with the name of the city on it. When I drink my morning coffee, I can reminisce about the blessings and perhaps ordeals of my travels.

At times, God prompts us to look back on our journey through loss so we will realize how far we've come. If we analyze yesterday or last week, we can get discouraged and believe we are making no headway. If we think about a longer period of time, we are better able to see that we *have* moved forward. We *have* changed. This long-term reflection helps us see our progress and God's provision and encourages us to continue our healing journey.

I first realized this while participating in Divorce Care for the second time. The first time I was very raw emotionally and had to fight off the tears and anger before, during, and after every meeting. I shared too much about my ex-husband's actions and not enough about my own responsibilities and recovery. I skipped the weeks covering the topics of forgiveness and reconciliation, and frequently felt more emotionally drained when I left than when I had arrived.

A year later, after I began attending the group again, I realized I was different. I no longer exhausted myself by holding back the tears; I processed and verbalized openly (with a few tears). I no longer felt heavy with despair because I was thinking about all the hard work ahead. Instead, I felt confident in my abilities to take on future challenges. Of course, I knew I had more progress to make, but this time of reminiscing in the group proved to be helpful and healing.

———

Then they cried out to the LORD in their trouble, and he brought them out of their distress. . . . Let the one who is wise heed these things and ponder the loving deeds of the LORD. (Ps. 107:28, 43)

Talking to God

"Father, guard my heart as I reflect on the past. Reveal to me the progress I have made and Your provision all along the way. Thank You, God, for Your constant presence, love, and guidance on this journey."

Journaling with God

In what ways do I feel stuck today?

In what ways have I progressed in my healing journey?

In what ways have I seen God at work in my life during this time?

How has God brought me through a trial in the past?

Which situation in Psalm 107 can I relate to most? How does seeing how God supplies the need in that situation give me hope?

FINDING HEALING IN PSALM 107

Read Psalm 107 and determine whether the trouble was self-inflicted or due to external circumstances. Also, note whether the cause changes God's response.

Seeking God First—The Wrong Place

But one thing I do: Forgetting what is behind and straining
toward what is ahead, I press on toward the goal to win the
prize for which God has called me heavenward in Christ Jesus.
(Phil. 3:13–14)

It was the second week of the semester. I walked into my college class-room ready to teach, and as I was unpacking my bag, I sensed unnatural stillness and the eyes of the students on me. I glanced up, smiled, and then quickly lowered my gaze thinking, *Oh no! I don't remember anybody's name.* One student said with a slight smirk, "Um . . . I think you are in the wrong room." I froze. Indeed I was. (I did teach in that classroom, but on a different day.) While I was relieved that I hadn't forgotten everybody's name, I was utterly embarrassed. In spite of their friendly offer to let me stay, I laughed and exited as quickly as possible.

I think we have all mistakenly walked into the wrong restroom—and made a quick about-face at the sight of a urinal. Intending to come to my house for Bible study for the second time, my friend Diane knocked on a door and *walked into the wrong house.* Fortunately, there was no threatening dog to greet her and the young boy she encountered was more concerned about the threat in his video game than in his home, so she escaped without repercussions.

In the above situations, we were in the wrong place, and once we real-ized the mistake, we did not linger—we fled. It would have been strange, even disturbing, for me to stay and try to teach to the wrong class, for us to use the wrong facilities (unless desperate), and for Diane to sit on the couch of a stranger's home awaiting the arrival of the others.

In the same way, it is disturbing, even harmful, if we relive, replay, or repeat the negative events and emotions of the past. We are, in effect, going to the wrong place. Our forward progress toward a better place, the place where God wants us to be, is impeded by our dwelling in the old place.

While recovering from divorce, it is easy to become consumed by regrets, guilt, and if-only laments. Certainly, reflection and self-evaluation are necessary for growth, but then we must leave our past behind to move forward.

———

Forget the former things; do not dwell on the past. See, I am
doing a new thing! Now it springs up; do you not perceive it? I
am making a way in the wilderness and streams in the wasteland.
(Isa. 43:18–19)

Talking to God

"Lord, forgive me for dwelling on the past, for replaying in my mind the wrongs done to me and the wrongs I have done. Help me to look to the future with You and to believe my past does not define me."

Journaling with God

What regrets from my past, especially concerning my marriage and divorce, do I keep replaying in my mind?

What steps do I need to take to move beyond my past and leave my regret and guilt at the foot of the cross?

What do I fear as I look toward the future? What am I looking forward to?

What safe person in my life could I ask to gently remind me when I get stuck in the past or the wrong place?

Day 4

FINDING HEALING IN PSALM 107

Read Psalm 107 and note the common theme in the first and last verses.

Seeking God First—View from the Floor

Then my soul will rejoice in the LORD and delight in his salvation.
(Ps. 35:9)

My students sit in desks arranged in semi-neat rows. If several students suddenly rejected the confines of their desks and sat on the floor, I'd probably stop midsentence and ask what was wrong. This is exactly what happened to my friend Leonard Lee, who trains pastors overseas.

He was in India teaching from Ephesians 2:4–5: "But because of his great love for us, God, who is rich in mercy, made us alive with Christ even when we were dead in transgressions—it is by grace you have been saved." Suddenly, several men pushed their chairs back from the table and sat cross-legged on the ground, eyes still attentive. Leonard probably wondered: *Have I offended them? Is this some kind of protest? Is that a signal that they need a bathroom break?* Offering a whole new perspective, his translator explained that their response to hearing a life-changing truth was to "sit on it."

I heard of another change in perspective on a radio interview. Lysa TerKeurst, author of *Unglued: Making Wise Choices in the Midst of Raw Emotions*, described an incident of raw emotions when her virus-laden laptop crashed. Panicking because she hadn't backed up the manuscript she was working on, she pleaded for help from a computer expert. Fortunately, the expert was able to retrieve most of her files and transfer them to an external hard drive. Lysa, of course, bought a new laptop so she could keep on working; however, soon after the purchase was made the laptop was stolen. She thought back to her previous computer crash and realized the circumstance that she had once viewed as extremely frustrating, she

107

now considered a blessing. If she hadn't previously transferred her files to the external hard drive, all would have been lost.

Often I need to broaden my perspective to consider God's sovereignty and love, especially when I'm frustrated or discouraged. Maybe my current trial, whether large or small, will somehow save me from a bigger disaster. Perhaps something good will come from my temporary pain. Probably somebody's reaction to what I said didn't mean what I initially thought. And certainly my words may have influence beyond what I realize in the moment.

Hope needs the correct perspective. We need to look beyond what is so readily visible and see the glorious work of God in our lives.

————

Now faith is confidence in what we hope for and assurance about what we do not see. (Heb. 11:1)

Talking to God

"Father God, I so often fail to have Your perspective. I see the glass half empty, focusing on the negative, ignoring the potential. Forgive me. Help me to have hope, to believe in Your goodness and Your attentive care in my life."

Journaling with God

On what recent event has my perspective changed from negative to positive?

In what areas of my life do I struggle to be hopeful? In what areas is my hope strong?

How can changing my perspective increase my hope?

How might giving thanks, exalting, and praising God, as the writer of Psalm 107 does, help me stay hopeful?

Finding Hope in the Story of the Feeding of Five Thousand (Luke 9:1–6, 10–17)

While traveling from town to town with His disciples, Jesus was healing diseases, casting out demons, and inviting people to follow Him. Eventually, He gave the disciples power and authority to do the same, as can be seen in verses 1–6. Then He asks them to do something new: feed five thousand people. Read the passage and let it give you hope in seemingly impossible situations.

Why do you think Jesus asks the disciples to give the crowd something to eat in verse 13?

What do you notice about the contrast between the disciples' perspective and Jesus's perspective on the situation?

What do you see as important about the *way* Jesus provided the food? What did He do? What did He not do?

How is this provisional miracle relevant to the circumstances of your own life?

Chapter 9

Seeking God for Our New Identity

Psalm of the Week: Psalm 8

Day 1

FINDING HEALING IN PSALM 8

Read Psalm 8, another one by David, and praise God for who He is. We better understand our own identity when we more clearly comprehend God's identity.

Seeing God's Heart

My daughter in whom I delight,

You are My beloved daughter, precious and priceless. You are worth more than all the treasures on earth. You are worth the life of My Son, Jesus.

You often do not see yourself that way, however. You look in the mirror and see flaws—imperfect skin, wrinkles, extra pounds. It saddens Me to see your self-criticism and shame. You frequently compare yourself to other daughters, believing you are not as valuable or lovable. You think I am more pleased with them, which is not true.

I do not view you through the lens of your past mistakes or your imperfections. I see you as pure, perfect, and beautiful. You are My wonderful creation, a work of art, purposed for a unique plan that only you can fulfill.

Reject the harmful labels others have placed on you or that you have placed on yourself. Instead, believe the loving words I have spoken to you and embrace your whole being as My awesome creation. Seek Me earnestly, and I will satisfy your soul. Peace and contentment will be yours when you fully embrace your identity as a child of Mine.

Your loving Creator

Talking to God

"Father God, You know I battle against those negative thoughts and labels daily. They slip in so easily, and bring me to despair if I do not remain on guard against them. I have to do more than keep them at bay, though. I have to replace them with Your truth. Open my eyes to see myself as You see me."

Journaling with God

What are three negative labels I have accepted as the truth about myself?

How has accepting these labels affected my life?

Knowing that God delights in me helps me create what new labels?

Instead of _____ I am _____.

Instead of _____ I am _____.

Instead of _____ I am _____.

Psalm 63:1 says, "You, God, are my God, earnestly I seek you; I thirst for you, my whole being longs for you, in a dry and parched land where there is no water." How might a deeper understanding of my true identity help me pray this same prayer?

FINDING HEALING IN PSALM 8

Read Psalm 8 out loud. Wherever David has written *mankind, human beings,* or *them,* insert *I* or *me,* respectively.

Seeking God First—Noise

My soul is weary with sorrow; strengthen me according to your word. (Ps. 119:28)

In the movie *The Fugitive,* Dr. Richard Kent, a renowned physician in Chicago, is wrongly convicted of the murder of his wife. The bus transporting him to prison crashes, and he escapes. While on the run, he calls his relentless pursuer, Deputy Gerard, to proclaim his innocence, which was real. He hangs up before the call can be traced, and the frustrated deputy yells, "Give me something!" The detectives deliver by isolating a sound on the audio of the phone call. It is the "L" train, and that identification indicates that the doctor is still in Chicago. The pursuit continues.

While not nearly as simple and speedy as Hollywood portrays, forensic audio experts can improve the quality of audio recordings in one of two ways: (1) by removing unwanted noise, and (2) by increasing the intelligibility of speech.

As we seek to recognize and understand God's voice, we can apply the same techniques: remove unwanted noise from the world and tune in to God's voice. The noise in the midst of our chaos can be distracting and confusing, even hurtful. We can listen to those depressing voices in our heads—*I'll never get over this; I'm unlovable; I've ruined my kids*—or we can listen to the Holy Spirit. He speaks of love and healing through Scripture, prayer, a friend, nature, a metaphor, or even a song.

My sheep listen to my voice; I know them, and they follow me.
(John 10:27)

Talking to God

"Lord, help me to block out unwanted noise and focus on Your voice. Help me to ignore Satan's hating voice that causes me to fear, and focus on Your loving voice that inspires me to love. Teach me to be still and listen to Your voice tell me who I am, and lead me further along the path of healing."

Journaling with God

What wrong voices have I listened to in the past?

How has listening to those voices shaped my identity?

What reassuring words about who I am would God speak to me this week?

FINDING HEALING IN PSALM 8

Read Psalm 8 and underline the verse you find most amazing.

Seeking God First—Unfinished Projects

*See what great love the Father has lavished on us, that we should be
called children of God! (1 John 3:1)*

I confess. My middle name could be Queen of Unfinished Projects or
Master of Good Intentions or simply Great Start! I am surrounded by
partially read books, unframed photos, blank walls, clothing in need of
mending . . .

If a button comes off an item of my daughter's clothing, I proclaim, "I
can fix that!" "Yeah, but you never get around to it" is her retort. (I beg
to differ on the "never" part. I distinctly recall a buttonless pair of white
shorts that I fixed within three short hours of the request last summer,
and it was only her second request.)

We ourselves are unfinished "projects"—yet finished at the same time.
We are finished in that the Lord has declared us pure, holy, forgiven, and
unconditionally loved. "For it is by grace you have been saved, through
faith—and this is not from yourselves, it is the gift of God—not by works,
so that no one can boast" (Eph. 2:8–9).

We are unfinished in that God is still at work in us, developing our
character and perfecting our faith through trials. Thankfully, the pain of
our circumstances can be the catalyst for a stronger relationship with God
as we depend on Him. Children of God do not escape trials, but we can
experience His gentle touch and comfort in the midst of them.

———

*He who began a good work in you will carry it on to completion
until the day of Christ Jesus. (Phil. 1:6)*

Talking to God

"God I don't like this trial. I am tired of feeling pain and just want it to stop. Please come alongside me and help me just as a good parent would help a struggling child. Thank You that I am Your child!"

Journaling with God

In what areas am I most vulnerable to feeling like an unfinished project? Am I trusting God to bring about change in me?

List five things a good parent would do for a hurting child.

Am I confident I am God's child? Why or why not? (If you are unsure of how to answer this, or if you'd like to have this confidence, see appendix B.)

How can the knowledge that I am a child of God help me during this time?

FINDING HEALING IN PSALM 8

Read Psalm 8 and observe our relationship to the rest of God's creation.

Seeking God First—Come Talk to Me

For the LORD takes delight in his people. (Ps. 149:4)

"Who is this Rebecca person?" Through the grapevine I heard that somebody was inquiring about me at my new job before I had even started.

My mind immediately skewed negative: *They think I don't deserve the job. They are all wondering why I was hired. I'm not good enough for the job, and I'm going to fail!* Any positive interpretation of how my name came up only flitted across my mind. It didn't land.

I walked into the office of my former boss, a brilliant woman and dear friend, without whom I wouldn't be where I am today. As I told her my story and expressed my fears, she smiled and shook her head, amused at my lack of confidence. She said, "You will be absolutely fine, and it won't be long before everybody appreciates you."

"Well, I don't know about *that*. You know me and how I think. I'm just not sure."

Still smiling, she replied, "I do know. So whenever you're feeling this way, come talk to me."

Two days later I realized the significance of her response. God speaks to us in this same encouraging way. "Becky, whenever you feel insecure, come talk to Me.

"Whenever you feel incapable, incompetent, inadequate, come talk to Me. Whenever you feel ugly, unworthy, unlovable, come talk to Me. Whenever you think you are a failure, hopeless, insignificant, come talk to Me.

"I enjoy impressing on your heart and mind how precious, valuable, and beautiful you are. Let your mind be so full of My truth about who you are that those lies have nowhere to land. Come talk to Me."

———

Are not five sparrows sold for two pennies? Yet not one of them is forgotten by God. Indeed, the very hairs of your head are all numbered. Don't be afraid; you are worth more than many sparrows. (Luke 12:6–7)

Talking to God

"God, help me to remember and embrace what You say I am instead of my own negative self-talk or the lies told to me. You have created me to be strong, capable, and valuable. Thank You for making me who I am today."

Journaling with God

What are five of my positive attributes?

What is one challenge I will face in the near future? What are my concerns about this challenge?

What encouraging words would God say to me about meeting this challenge?

How does knowing that the Creator of the universe is mindful of me (Ps. 8:4) help me better appreciate my worth?

Finding Hope in Who God Says We Are

Who we are, or more accurately, who we *believe* we are, dramatically affects our decisions, emotions, relationships, dreams, and just about every other aspect of our lives. Therefore, we need to more fully understand and embrace who God says we are, especially in this time when self-doubt and self-condemnation abound.

Read the following verses. Note what the verses say about our identity. Then comment on what it would mean to fully live out this identity.

Genesis 1:27
Isaiah 64:8
John 1:12
John 15:15
2 Corinthians 5:17
Ephesians 1:4
Ephesians 2:10
Ephesians 5:8
Philippians 3:20
1 Peter 2:9
1 John 3:1–3

With which identity are you the most comfortable? Why?

Which identity is the most difficult to accept? Why?

For which identity are you the most thankful? Spend some time thanking God for who He has made you to be.

Chapter 10

Seeking God for Intimacy

Psalm of the Week: Psalm 139

Day 1

FINDING HEALING IN PSALM 139

Read Psalm 139, which was written by David. Consider how well and how long God has known David.

Seeing God's Heart

My dear child,

How are you today? How are you really? I want you to tell Me without pretense, without walls, without hesitation. Just be you in My presence.

Reconciling My power and majesty with My love and tenderness can be a challenge at times, I know. *How can the Creator of the universe desire a personal relationship?* you wonder. *How can this be?* It's by design. I created you to be a relational being, to have close, intimate relationships with others. I have also designed you to have an intimate relationship with Me.

Intimacy involves detailed knowledge and deep understanding of each other. Talk to Me about anything, even if you are angry with Me. Share your wildest hopes, your deepest fears. Talk to Me throughout the day, not just in moments of crisis, for I am always with you, waiting to experience life together.

I want you to have intimate knowledge of Me as well, so I have given you My truth in Scripture. This truth is not a list of rules to limit your life, nor is it a bunch of facts to fill your head with information *about* Me. I have gifted you with the Word of God; nature; miracles; my Son, Jesus; and the Holy Spirit—all so you can deeply comprehend and experience who I am and how much I love you.

Intimacy also involves affection. I delight in you. I want to spend time with you. I want to wrap My arms around you to comfort you and convince you of your lovability and value. I want to see you smile. Can you feel My loving presence?

I invite you to delight in Me as well. Rejoice in My creation, celebrate My love, discover My character, rest in My goodness.

Your loving Creator

Talking to God

"Dear Father, intimacy with You is a mystery to me, exciting and amazing but sometimes confusing. I do desire to know You better, to walk closer with You, but sometimes I don't truly grasp how to do it. Help me to understand this mystery, and show me how to walk more intimately with You every day."

Journaling with God

Which sentence of the letter most encouraged me and why?

How do I feel about developing intimacy with God?

What is one thing I can commit to doing regularly in order to create more intimacy with God?

My favorite verse from Psalm 139 is _____ because _____.

FINDING HEALING IN PSALM 139

Read Psalm 139 and circle all the verbs that describe how God knows us (for example, v. 1, *have searched* and *know*).

Seeking God First—Starfish

How precious to me are your thoughts, God! How vast is the sum of them! (Ps. 139:17)

I don't have a starfish story. Stasi Eldredge does.

Stasi writes in her book *Captivating* of a time when she was walking on a beach alone, seeking a special, personal sign that God loved her. Her husband, John, had told her he had seen a whale breach right in front of him at a time when the whale migration had long since passed. This was a gift for John's heart alone, and Stasi longed for the same. So she prayed for a whale.

Instead, she saw a starfish, a beautiful orange starfish nestled in a serene tide pool. God knew Stasi was more interested in this delicate and calming creature than in an overwhelmingly large whale. Then she rounded the corner. There she saw *hundreds* of starfish—a gift for her heart.

She rejoiced. "God didn't just love me. He LOOOOVED me! Intimately, personally, completely."[9]

Do I really believe God knows and loves us so much that He gives us little gifts like starfish? Can we be so bold as to ask for them?

I have been asking, praying, thinking, reading past journal entries—trying to find my own starfish story for this devotional. To be honest, I couldn't find one. Did I miss it? Do I not open my eyes enough to see the personal, intimate ways in which God shows His love toward me?

Yes, I can find plenty of answers to prayer, often just in time or in ways I didn't expect. I can remember many times when God provided friends or family to support me when I needed it. I can recall God speaking to me

121

through Bible passages to soothe my spirit and soul. I am so grateful for all of these times, but I can't recall a starfish story, a story in which God orchestrates a seemingly trivial detail, just for me.

I realize that one of the reasons I can't identify such a story is because I have a hard time accepting that level of love, of intimacy from God. It makes me squirm. It seems too much for me to ask or expect. But this painful road of divorce, the most difficult ordeal of my life, has awakened my heart to seek God. I want to know Him more deeply, to follow Him more closely, to praise Him more expressively.

And I want to see some starfish. I want to see God in the details, to experience His affections for me, to sense His delight in me. I want to more fully believe He LOOOOVES me!

Do you want a starfish story?

_____

Your Father knows what you need before you ask him. (Matt. 6:8)

Talking to God

"Father God, I know in my head that You love me, but I know there's more. Teach me to understand that You are a personal God, eager to express Your tender love toward me in special, intimate ways. Open my eyes to see and be thankful for the many ways You've loved and cared for me during this season—and to see some starfish."

Journaling with God

In what ways has God shown His care for me this week?

Is it easy or difficult for me to accept this intimate care and love from God? Why?

How can recognizing God's intimate knowledge of me and love for me affect my life?

FINDING HEALING IN PSALM 139

Read Psalm 139 out loud and underline anything that stands out to you.

Seeking God First—Potlucks

For it is by grace you have been saved, through faith—and this is not from yourselves, it is the gift of God—not by works, so that no one can boast. (Eph. 2:8–9)

I rushed to the church straight from work, feeling guilty and inadequate because I was going to a potluck empty-handed—and this was not the first time. *I should have brought something homemade. Or at least I should have gone to the store for a vegetable platter or chips and dip. Why don't I ever plan ahead?*

Granted, this was a potluck for a hundred people, and one less green bean casserole, bowl of garlic mashed potatoes, or decadent, chocolate layer cake would not have been missed—okay, maybe the chocolate cake. Fighting the temptation to go home, I snuck into the room and settled quickly in a seat, hiding my empty hands and guilt. I took a deep breath and relaxed as I observed people shuffling dishes to try to make all the food fit on the tables, and I realized that they didn't even notice that I hadn't contributed, much less judge me for it.

Besides, offering up the "I didn't have any food" excuse to justify my absence would have met with resounding protests from my friends. After confessing my misstep to my friend Valerie, she responded, "Don't worry about it! I'm just glad you're here."

God also simply desires our presence. We *have to* come to him empty-handed and recognize that we can do nothing to earn the privilege of receiving His favor, mercy, grace, and love. I have often operated under the misguided notion that I have to earn my way by serving Him and others with good works. The pressure to do so intensified after my divorce because I felt I had failed God and those closest to me in so many ways, and I needed to make up for it. But I was broken and empty, with no energy or ability to contribute. I had nothing to bring to God.

But Jesus paid the price for all my sins and afforded me the honor of standing in God's presence; I could never earn the privilege, even on my best day. Now, as I approach God's throne of grace, I realize that He is somehow simultaneously whispering and cheering, "Becky, I'm just glad you're here."

———

In him and through faith in him we may approach God with freedom and confidence. (Eph. 3:12)

Talking to God

"Lord, help me remember that You embrace me with unconditional love, and assure me that I may enter into Your presence despite my brokenness and inadequacies. As I rest in Your presence, reveal Your wonderful ways to me so that I may know You more intimately."

Journaling with God

Do I believe I have to earn God's love through good works?

Do I also believe I have to earn others' love through my actions? How has this affected my life?

How can I change my approach to God and develop more intimacy with Him?

Seeking God First—The Real Me

I have summoned you by name; you are mine. (Isa. 43:1)

He called on me, but I chickened out.

At a Youth for Christ high school retreat workshop, the speaker asked us to close our eyes and imagine ourselves as the center of attention, standing in the middle of a crowded room with all eyes focused on us. What were we wearing? What were the people thinking about us? What were we feeling in that moment? Then we noticed Jesus in the crowd; He was also looking at us. What did He think about us? Then what did we feel?

After more questions and promptings for details, the speaker asked us to open our eyes and share what we had imagined. A few kids shared, but not many. This was high school after all and most didn't want to damage their cool facade.

Then it happened—the eye contact, followed by, "Rebecca, what did you see?" I couldn't even talk. I just shook my head, and I've regretted it to this day.

I now realize I avoided sharing not just because I was shy but because I was emotional, and crying would have reinforced my nerdy, awkward image. Even so, I wish I had spoken up and told my story. I wish I had explained that I was wearing a wedding dress and standing on a pedestal while people milled around me in that crowded room. Situationally, I was the focal point of the room, but in fact, I received only a few casual glances. After finding nothing noteworthy or special about me, people quickly returned to their conversations. Then I realized I was invisible to them—I was actually hidden inside a statue of me in a wedding dress. I couldn't get out—or maybe I didn't want to get out.

Then I saw Jesus. His eyes locked onto mine, seeing past the statue shell to the real me inside. I couldn't hide from His scrutiny, but then I realized I didn't want to or need to. He was safe and peaceful. He didn't use words, but His eyes spoke kindness and love into my soul. I was worthy of His attention. All of me was known and loved. Jesus looked past my facade and outward appearances to see the real me, special and beautiful.

This reminds me of Psalm 139:1, 14 where David prays, "You have searched me, LORD, and you know me. . . . I praise you because I am fearfully and wonderfully made." The fact that God knows us so well used to bother me, but now I find comfort in God's all-knowing scrutiny, especially when I feel broken. He sees all of me, but I no longer fear His judgment because I am "fearfully and wonderfully made."

You have searched me, LORD, and you know me. . . . You are familiar with all my ways. (Ps. 139:1, 3)

Talking to God

"Dear God, it is difficult to fathom that the Lord of the universe even considers me and all my ways. Help me to understand and embrace Your constant presence and loving intimacy. Show me more of who You are so that I may become familiar with *Your* ways."

Journaling with God

How does realizing that God knows me completely make me feel?

How convinced am I that I am "fearfully and wonderfully made"? How does this knowledge affect my life?

How does my past affect how God sees me?

How do I think God sees me today?

Finding Hope in God's Intimate Knowledge of Us (Ps. 139)

In his prayer to God, David, the writer of this psalm, rejoices in God's intimate creation and knowledge of him. Even if you are familiar with the psalm, try reading it with fresh eyes and embrace the wonder that the Creator of all the earth is familiar with every part of us. And if He knows *everything* about us, He knows our struggles, our tears, our despairing thoughts. Read the psalm and gain comfort from God's intimate knowledge of you.

After reading Psalm 139, what did you learn about God's knowledge of the psalmist? How does David respond to this knowledge? What is your response to God's knowledge of you?

What stands out to you in this psalm about how we were made? What is David's response? What is your response?

At the end of the psalm, what does David invite God to do? After reading this psalm, what is your invitation to God?

How does the awareness of how much God knows you affect your perspective on your current struggles?

Chapter 11

Seeking God for Our Joy

Psalm of the Week: Psalm 30

FINDING HEALING IN PSALM 30

Read Psalm 30 and note what David says God has done for him.

Seeing God's Heart

My precious child,

Joy may seem impossible right now, but trust Me when I say you can experience true joy again.

The joy I offer you is not fleeting happiness based on changeable circumstances. It cannot be snatched away by others. It is not based on what you do or don't do.

My joy resides deep in your soul and fills you with peace and fulfillment. The joy I offer you is based on our relationship. Joy comes from constant assurance of My love for you and from knowing I have a purposeful plan for your life. Joy comes from participating with Me in loving others.

To more fully experience this joy, delight in Me as I delight in you. As the deer pants for water, seek after Me, for in My presence is where you will find joy. I stand at the door and knock, not just to offer salvation but also to offer a healing, intimate touch at the core of your being.

Abide in Me, and I will fill you with songs of joy no matter what your current circumstances are. I have done great things for you and will give you even more gifts if you will truly welcome them.

Please open the door, invite Me in, and accept My gift.

Jesus, your Lord

Talking to God

"Jesus, thank You for the gift of joy. I know I often leave that gift unopened as I focus on my circumstances and my imperfections. Help me to rest in Your love for me and embrace Your goodness to me, for I know that is where my joy lies."

Journaling with God

What is my definition of joy?

Do I believe joy is possible right now? Why or why not?

What invitation should I extend to Jesus?

Which verse in Psalm 30 best fits what God has done for me recently?

FINDING HEALING IN PSALM 30

Read Psalm 30 out loud and underline the verse that best describes you today and the verse you most hope will describe you in the future (it could be the same verse).

Seeking God First—Talk to Her

If you keep my commands, you will remain in my love, just as I have kept my Father's commands and remain in his love. I have told you this so that my joy may be in you and that your joy may be complete. (John 15:10–11)

I sidestep down a row of seats at church and sit down, leaving a socially appropriate empty seat between me and another woman. Part of me wishes I had just stayed home in isolation, stewing in my mood du jour, but I think I can avoid any interaction because I go to such a large church. While waiting for the service to begin, I peruse the extensive bulletin. *You should talk to that woman.* After a brief glance at the woman with no ensuing recognition, I return to the bulletin, ignoring my ubiquitous "should" thoughts.

Talk to her.

God? Is that You or Ms. Should?

Talk to her.

Really, God? You know the emotional state I'm in; I'm barely holding it together. I don't want to talk to anybody right now. Plus, I'm an introvert. Remember, You made me that way. Small talk is awkward for me, even when I'm in a good mood. And I'm not in a good mood, in case You missed that point.

Talk to her.

Okay, but I need Your help.

I steal a longer glance and hope I can force a smile when we make eye contact. She stares straight ahead, jaw clenched. *Hmm. I know that look. She seems to be barely holding it together.* I start to say something, but the music begins, and the opportunity passes. *Later, I promise.*

Later is almost too late, but I finally strike up a conversation as we are walking out the door. She takes a long look at me and says I look familiar. We go through the usual round of questions to determine where our paths have crossed in the past until we realize we were in the same young couples Bible study over *twenty-five* years ago. Further conversation reveals that we are both separated from our husbands.

Wow. In Your infinite wisdom and love, God, You seat us next to each other in a worship center that seats two thousand people.

We linger in the parking lot, and I listen more than I talk because her separation is much more recent than mine, her emotions more raw. We make tentative plans for lunch, exchange phone numbers, and promise to pray for each other.

As I drive home, I suddenly wonder what happened to the self-absorbed, miserable woman who drove this car to church. The current driver is lighter, at peace, joyful even. Of course, I am saddened by my friend's situation, but I am joyful that God was able to use me in some small way to help her feel less alone and more understood. And I'm grateful that God comforted me in the process.

———

Praise be to the God and Father of our Lord Jesus Christ,
the Father of compassion and the God of all comfort, who
comforts us in all our troubles, so that we can comfort those in
any trouble with the comfort we ourselves receive from God.
(2 Cor. 1:3–4)

Talking to God

"Lord, forgive me when I am so self-absorbed that I miss seeing those in pain around me. Thank You for the gift of joy when You use me and the pain of my circumstances to help others. I feel joy when I let Your gentle hand steer me to what is good, perfect, and pleasing in Your sight."

Journaling with God

What were the circumstances when I last comforted somebody? What did God teach me in that experience?

Why do we sometimes experience joy when we comfort others?

Who in my life needs comforting? What will I do this week to reach out to that person?

FINDING HEALING IN PSALM 30
Read Psalm 30 and note how David expressed his joy.

Seeking God First—Where's the Mustard?

If all must be right with the world before I have a fling with joy, I shall be somber forever. —Lewis Smedes

"Where's the mustard?" a teenage boy asks his mom.

"In the fridge," she responds, stating the obvious.

"*Where* in the fridge?"

"On the right side in the back."

"I don't see it."

She comes to his aid and finds the mustard in a millisecond.

Joseph T. Hallinan, in his book *Why We Make Mistakes*, explains why this scenario is repeatedly played out in every kitchen across America. We look, but we do not see. Hallinan describes an experiment where volunteers were asked to look at thousands of images with busy backgrounds to see if they could spot a tool such as a wrench or hammer—the mustard in the refrigerator. If the tool was often present in a set of images, the volunteers missed it only 7 percent of the time. If the tool was rarely present, they missed it 30 percent of the time. Why? If it was a rare find, they gave up looking sooner. According to the researchers, "We are built—perhaps hardwired—to quit early when the target is unlikely to be there."[10]

I hate to admit it, but this is how I feel about joy when my heart is heavy. I think it will be hard to find, and I'm not sure if it is there at all. I have difficulty believing David when he says, "Those who sow with tears will reap with songs of joy" (Ps. 126:5).

Therefore, I have to look harder and not give up. I have to pursue joy more earnestly, more intentionally—beginning with small activities, such as laughing with friends, reading a good book, marveling at a beautiful sunset—to catch a glimpse of the deep joy God has made available for me.

What brings the most joy, of course, is drawing close to God and being in His will. There's no greater joy than participating with God in His wonderful plan for redemption and love in my life and the lives of those around me.

The temptation to stop looking for joy is almost overwhelming in the midst of trying circumstances. But when I press on toward God's presence, reflecting on His love and enjoying His gifts, I find joy—way in the back, behind the jar of pickles, the carton of milk, and the container of questionable leftovers. The search is well worth the effort.

———

You turned my wailing into dancing; you removed my sackcloth
and clothed me with joy, that my heart may sing your praises and
not be silent. LORD my God, I will praise you forever.
(Ps. 30:11–12)

Talking to God

"Lord, help me to believe in Your promises of joy and not to give up looking. Protect me from settling for counterfeit joy apart from You. May I find true joy in Your presence, despite my circumstances or emotions, which vary from one day to the next."

Journaling with God

Is it easy for me to find joy? Why or why not?

What are five activities that bring me joy? Which one will I commit to doing this week?

What was I doing the last time I felt joy?

How can I cultivate joy despite difficult circumstances?

FINDING HEALING IN PSALM 30
Read Psalm 30 and memorize your favorite verse.

Seeking God First—The List

I will give thanks to you, LORD, with all my heart; I will tell of all your wonderful deeds. (Ps. 9:1)

My friend Sue, her husband, Tom, and their two young boys began their fourth day of a wonderfully restful houseboat vacation on the Lake of the Ozarks. A storm came up, however, so they headed to shore. At the dock Tom steered and Sue went out on the deck with her younger son, Jonathon, to secure the boat to the dock. She thought about letting her son tie the boat but opted to do it herself, thinking it might be too tricky in the relentless rain and wind.

As she held on to the rail with her left hand, the boat lurched upward in a strong swell, and an overhead piece of steel sliced off her left index finger. In shock and not yet feeling pain, she calmly wrapped her hand in a towel and told Jonathon to tell Daddy she lost her finger. She remembers how strange it felt to suddenly have a piece of her gone and how vulnerable she felt.

Her husband, then a pastor, told this story several times in his sermons, not for what happened on the boat but for what happened afterward in the hospital. Alone in her room, Sue compiled a long list of things for which she was thankful. She was grateful that her son was not injured, that it was her left hand and not her right, that the experienced trauma team treated her calmly and skillfully . . . and the list continued. What a powerful lesson in perspective and thankfulness to God she modeled for her two sons!

Through divorce, we have lost a piece of ourselves, and we often feel vulnerable—very vulnerable. However, we can still compile a list of things for which we are thankful. Perhaps we have gained a deeper appreciation for supportive friends and family members. We may have established new friendships and grown personally, neither of which we would have done without the trial of separation and divorce. Most importantly, perhaps we have strengthened our commitment to and relationship with God. As we express our thankfulness to God, we find peace, contentment, and, yes, even joy.

———

Give thanks in all circumstances; for this is God's will for you in Christ Jesus. (1 Thess. 5:18)

Talking to God

"Lord, often I am not grateful at all in my current circumstances. I complain, condemn, and cry bitterly, ignoring Your goodness. Renew my mind and let thoughts of Your tender faithfulness and love transform my perspective."

Journaling with God

What is the most devastating loss I have suffered as a result of my separation or divorce?

In what ways do I feel vulnerable?

What five things am I thankful for that have occurred because of this separation or divorce?

What five attributes of God am I especially thankful for during this difficult time?

Finding Hope in the Story of the Suffering Church
(1 Peter 1:1–9)

First Peter is an epistle, a letter written to Christians in the early church. In it, Peter speaks enthusiastically of God's grace and salvation, but he never tells his readers that because they believe in Jesus life will be care-free. The early Christians often experienced persecution, yet Peter challenged them to be holy and filled with joy because of their suffering for Christ. Even though suffering because of persecution is different from suffering because of divorce, the same principle for our faith holds true. We must focus on Christ, obey with holy living, and receive joy in the midst of suffering.

Read the passage.

Who is writing the letter, and to whom is it written (vv. 1–2)?

In verses 3 through 5, Peter mentions several of the gifts we have been given. What specific details, if any, does Peter offer about each gift?

Mercy	Inheritance
New birth	Shielded
Hope	Salvation

Why are these gifts particularly important for the suffering, persecuted Christian?

Which of these gifts brings you the most encouragement, hope, or joy?

What are the characteristics of faith described in verses 6 through 9? How would you describe your own faith during this trial?

Read through the passage again and insert *me* or *I* for every *us* and *you*. What do you think about the concept of joy in the midst of your own suffering?

Chapter 12

Seeking God for Our Next Steps

Psalm of the Week: Psalm 121

Day 1

FINDING HEALING IN PSALM 121
Read Psalm 121 out loud and circle any repeated expressions.

Seeing God's Heart

My faithful child,

I'm so proud of you for all the ways you've grown during this difficult time. I know you sometimes feel stuck in the same patterns and feelings and wonder how long it will take to feel normal again. I know the journey is long, slow, and painful, but you're moving! Even working through this book shows you are moving. You're making steady progress in this journey to the new life I have planned for you!

Don't listen to the enemy who says you haven't progressed enough, that you should be over this crisis by now. I've begun a good work in you, and you *have* progressed, more than you realize. You're looking more to the future than the past. You're building yourself a new identity, recognizing your unique gifts and worth. You're learning that change can be good.

Trust that I've worked miracles in your life. Look for little ways you react differently or think differently, and be grateful for small victories. Listen to those supportive friends and family members who say you've changed, that you look more alive, that you've come a long way. I've placed specific people in your life to build you up, so look for them and accept their affirmations. Also, be cognizant of those who do not have your best interests in mind and reject their discouraging words.

Most importantly, you've drawn closer to Me, your heavenly Father, and I so delight in your presence! I rejoice when you allow Me into your life to wipe your tears, hold your hand, show you hope, and walk by your side in every circumstance. Nothing can separate us now; nothing will separate us in the future.

The work I've begun in you isn't finished, of course. But instead of bemoaning how much more there is to do, celebrate My great patience and grace! Claim My promise; say, "My God is not finished with me yet!" And then just *be*. Be My daughter and rest in My pleasure and peace. Be thankful, knowing I am good and My love endures forever.

After all, you are My child, wonderfully and beautifully made. In you, I delight!

     Your loving Father

Talking to God

"Lord, growing and changing is difficult, and I haven't always worked very diligently at it. At times, I've wanted to stay in my metaphorical hospital bed and let my muscles atrophy, but You didn't let me. You made me get up and walk, and I'm so grateful! I now live in sweet expectation of experiencing Your immeasurable goodness in each step of my journey to wholeness."

Journaling with God

What positive comments have I received from others about my recovery or growth?

In what two areas do I see the most growth in myself over the past few months?

How can I just be with God and delight in His presence?

What is my understanding of the phrase *watch over* from Psalm 121?

FINDING HEALING IN PSALM 121

Read Psalm 121 and observe the writer's confidence in God.

Seeking God First—How Long?

The righteous choose their friends carefully. (Prov. 12:26)

After a wonderful meal at a friend's house, I received a man's offer to walk me to my car. Granted, the country property was pretty dark, but I didn't really see the need for an escort for the one-hundred-foot walk. I shrugged, thinking, *Well, okay. That's nice, I guess. Wait! What does that really mean? Is he simply being polite and protective, or does he want to ask me out?* I took no chances. I started walking fast, waved that I was fine, and bolted to my car. Then I felt stupid, awkward, and juvenile. During the drive home I laughed at myself but also acknowledged something important: I still wasn't ready to date.

In the beginning stages of my divorce, the thought of dating, if it crossed my mind at all, made me laugh, cry, roll my eyes, or shudder in terror. But others may see only the positive potential of a new relationship and want to begin dating as soon as possible. No matter where we fall on this spectrum, as we contemplate entering the dating world, we wonder *who* and *how* to date. Another key question is *when* to date. When will I be emotionally ready? When is it part of God's plan for me?

It's best if we've experienced significant growth and healing before we begin to date. If we rush into dating without first doing the hard work of healing after a broken marriage, our wounds remain. And we bring that sorrow and baggage into the new relationship. We also might need to deal with the deep inner-child wounds that were present before the marriage began. If we don't allow those deep hurts to surface and face them, we will repeat our past mistakes.

We may think finding somebody who loves us will heal our wounds and make us feel better about ourselves. *If only I weren't alone, I would be happy. I will heal when I find somebody who will love me as I am.* There's nothing wrong with desiring a relationship; God designed us as relational beings.

However, there is something wrong with depending on another person to make us feel valued or whole. If we don't have a sense of value and worth apart from a man, we won't have it with him, and we won't attract somebody who truly appreciates and loves us. Healthy people attract healthy people.

So how much healing is enough? Of course the answer is different for each person, but answering yes to the following questions may help you decide that you're ready to date:

Am I legally divorced?

Do I feel neutral about my ex-husband (no longer in love and no longer raging)?

Have I learned to find my self-worth and confidence in how God sees me?

Have I (re)discovered my voice and gifts?

Do I like myself?

Do I know myself enough to be confident in my boundaries and values?

Am I willing and able to give the time and emotional energy a new relationship needs?

Am I able to maintain my priority of following God in the midst of a new relationship?

Am I able to trust God with the outcome of a new relationship?

———

Be still before the LORD and wait patiently for him. (Ps. 37:7)

Talking to God

"Father God, grant me an extra measure of patience to wait for Your timing and Your leading. It's hard to wait. It's hard to be alone. Help me not to long for what I don't have but instead to focus on the hard work of healing and on drawing closer to You. I know that You are watching over me even in this area. I trust that Your will is the best for me, and I long to understand and obey that will."

Journaling with God

Which one of the pre-dating questions above can I most confidently say yes to and why?

Which question do I most decisively say no to and why? (Or which question am I not sure about?)

What fears do I have about dating? What am I looking forward to about dating?

Overall, do I think I am ready to date? Why or why not?

Read Psalm 121, underline the most assuring verse, and put a question mark by the most confusing verse.

Seeking God First—I Reckon

*If you want to become healthy, you have to surround yourself with
a group of people that are getting healthy, and you have to be
connected to a community that is doing what you want to do.*
—Henry Cloud, Safe People

One of my daughters is taking a class called Voice, Diction, and Dialects, and she regularly speaks in front of the class in an assigned, unnatural manner. One assignment was to speak in a southern drawl, so she practiced at a family dinner. She's not good at imitating accents, which is readily apparent to her and anybody else listening. After first teasing her mercilessly, as families tend to do, we tried to help her practice. We all sounded like desperate actors auditioning for the *Beverly Hillbillies*, beginning every sentence with "I reckon" and throwing in an occasional "Weeell, doggies," a few "over yonders," and a final "Y'all come back now, ya hear!"

When I started attending the singles community at my church, I felt like my daughter trying to speak in an accent that wasn't hers. I had to play a role that was unfamiliar, uncomfortable, and unwanted. I was tempted to retreat, to give up. I didn't feel I had the emotional energy, but I pressed on.

Going to the first meeting forced me to confront singleness as part of my new identity. To reinforce this new identity, the name tags we placed on our shirts displayed a large S for single. Well, not really, but that was how awkward I felt. Despite calling a friend to meet me there, I was self-conscious, wary, and emotional. Was this really worth it?

Unequivocally, YES!

I now have some fantastic single friends to walk with me as I adjust to single life. And I never would have met them if I hadn't taken the risk of going to the meeting. My motivation in going wasn't to find a date; my goal was to develop friendships with single people, both men and women, with whom I shared interests and values. These friends have been invaluable to me. They're teaching me to live life fully and to appreciate who I am.

Unfortunately, finding a friendly, safe singles group to become part of may take some work. Often churches are too small to have a singles group, and sometimes a group isn't healthy. Of course, you do not have to find a singles group, and you may already have some close, established friendships you can depend on. But consider opportunities for new friendships, and most importantly, avoid isolation, which prolongs the healing process.

This can be a time of great discovery of new relationships and new interests. Seek guidance from God, and be open-minded and creative in your search. Try a new interest group, find a place to volunteer and serve, take an art class, join a meetup group with a friend—whatever you need to do to become involved in community. And then be yourself.

――――

It is not good for . . . man to be alone. (Gen. 2:18)

Talking to God

"Lord, You have made us relational beings, so we need other people in our lives. Give me the desire and boldness to meet new people or to deepen old friendships instead of isolating myself. You've promised to guide me if I ask, so I'm asking You to guide me now. Please help me find safe people who love You. Help me to be open to the friendships You have for me."

Journaling with God

Do I feel the need or desire to connect and interact more in community?

How am I currently feeling about my identity as a single woman? Does my feeling line up well with God's truth?

What am I looking forward to as I invest in new friendships?

How does the knowledge that the Lord is watching over me (Ps. 121) help me as I face my new identity?

FINDING HEALING IN PSALM 121

Read Psalm 121 and note the writer's statements about
God's character and power.

Seeking God First—Do You Want to Ride?

The glory of God is man fully alive. —Irenaeus

I love horses. Their majesty, strength, and beauty inspire me. I also love
God's invitations to us. His beckoning to follow, love, and know amazes
me. Perhaps these two loves explain why I am so captivated by the following story.

Allen Arnold, author of *The Story of With: A Better Way to Live, Love,
and Create*, tells the story of a vision God gave him as he was grappling
with a decision to uproot his family from a fantastic church community,
move across the country, and join a ministry at a lower salary:

> With eyes closed in prayer, I saw my wife and I walking along a
> forest trail. We came to a clearing with a small corral. Inside were
> two stallions. An old rancher stood on the opposite side with a
> boot propped on the rail, his cowboy hat slightly cocked. When
> he smiled, the skin creased around his steel-blue eyes. . . .
>
> The rancher asked in a gentle voice, "Do you want to ride?" . . .
>
> Only after we accepted the invitation did we realize there was
> a third horse in the stable. The offer was never to ride alone, but
> *with* Him.[11]

Do I want to ride? Yes! Do I want to go on an adventure with God? Yes!
But what does that mean I should do? What does that look like? Arnold
suggests that we find our true calling in relationship with God: "Spend
time with [God]. And see what the two of you will discover together on

146

the playground of possibilities. He may surprise you by inviting you into something you never imagined doing."[12]

This may mean we take time to remember our earlier dreams, figure out how God has uniquely gifted us, be brave enough to say yes to opportunities and open doors God places before us, and above all, enjoy intimacy with God along the journey.

Shonda Rhimes, creator and executive producer of *Grey's Anatomy*, *Private Practice*, and *Scandal*, describes her own openness to new adventures in her book *Year of Yes*. She committed to saying yes for an entire year to any invitation, especially terrifying ones that involved public speaking. Granted, seeking God's guidance and presence was not part of her adventure, but she sought growth, freedom, empowerment, and discovery. She found them. Her sister said to her, "And now you have completely transformed. You're alive. You're living. Some people never do that."[13] How much more alive and fulfilled could we be with God by our side!

What adventure does God have for us in our new lives? What should we say yes to and start exploring? I practiced exploring new opportunities when I said yes to learning how to play golf with a group of friends. Preferring not to publicly expose my inadequacies, I tend to avoid activities in which I have no skill, but I forced myself to go. It turns out I love golf! I've also forced myself to go to a relationship class, a singles community, and writers' conferences. I'm thinking of learning how to play Bridge next, and I am praying about an opportunity to go to Honduras on a summer mission trip.

A significant example of my saying yes to an opportunity God placed before me is writing this book. Again, I didn't feel competent, but God prepared the trail before me and rode alongside me each mile of this journey. The book, from conception to completion, has brought adventure, fulfillment, and mystery to my life. I don't know what will come along next, but I know I want to keep saying yes to God.

We are still healing. We may have financial issues. We might have relationship problems. But we also have freedom, more than we realize, to say yes, even to things that scare us. As we continue to say yes to God's promptings, we more fully become who God has made us to be.

Do you want to ride?

———

Do you not know that in a race all the runners run, but only one gets the prize? Run [ride] in such a way as to get the prize.
(1 Cor. 9:24)

Talking to God

"Lord, I am both anxious and thrilled about my life ahead. I feel as though I am emerging from darkness into light. While I know the days ahead will not be trouble free, even on adventures planned and blessed by You, I am ready to ride!"

Journaling with God

How open-minded am I to new adventures in my life? Do I see them as stressful or exciting?

What could God be calling me to say yes to right now?

How can I develop and maintain a spirit of anticipation for adventures with God?

What have I learned about God in this book so far that helps me look forward to the future?

Finding Hope in the Story of the Vine (John 15:1–17)

In John 14–17, John writes four chapters about Jesus's private instructions, promises, predictions, and prayers for His disciples. Jesus was preparing His disciples for His departure (John 13:33). Seeing Jesus, whom they had followed for years, crucified was going to be devastating. Their lives were going to change in ways they had never imagined. In John 15, Jesus explains that the key to a productive, fulfilling life is living close to God in all circumstances.

Read John 15:1–17.

As we continue to make imperfect progress in our healing journey and say yes to new adventures, our most important goal is to stay close to God.

Who do the vine, the gardener, and the branches represent?

What are the results of remaining in the vine and of not remaining in the vine?

What does it mean to remain in God's love?

Throughout the passage, what does Jesus say about bearing fruit? What does this mean in practical terms for your life?

What does it mean to you to be called God's friend?

Which verse has the greatest effect on you as you think about your relationship with God?

Appendix A
Group Guidelines

If you choose to work through this book as a group, I would suggest printing out and adhering to the following guidelines. They will help each group member feel safe as you share openly about sensitive issues and commit to this healing journey together in the presence of the Holy Spirit. (A free leader's guide with further information is available online at rebeccamitchellauthor.com.)

As group members, we commit to these principles:

1. *Confidentiality.* Whatever is shared in the group must stay within the group in order to establish trust and safety. We must guard the confidentiality of each woman zealously. This is of utmost importance.

2. *Acceptance of others.* We have different relational circumstances, varied experiences from our families of origin, and unique strengths and weaknesses that led us to where we are today. An obstacle that's relatively easy to face for one person may be overwhelmingly debilitating for another. One woman may battle depression for years, for example, while another never experiences depression or shakes it off after a few weeks. We commit to listening to each other share fully and to accepting, loving, and encouraging each other without judgment.

3. *Acceptance of ourselves.* In the same way, we must practice acceptance of ourselves. We can easily succumb to negative self-talk. We've all made mistakes—sometimes grievous ones—affecting those closest

to us, but the blood of Christ covers those mistakes, and we come to these meetings to move on in our lives, fully forgiven. Remember, there's nothing we can do to make God love us more, and there's nothing we can do to make God love us less.

4. *Vulnerability.* As we prepare a safe and loving atmosphere, we become vulnerable with each other and share deep wounds, fears, and sorrows. Tears are inevitable. We will sensitively allow time for everybody to share as fully as needed and resist the urge to offer advice too quickly. Sometimes we can offer helpful insights of how we dealt with a similar struggle; most times we'll need to just listen and lift up our sister in prayer.

   Also, we recognize that sharing passionately about our pain is different from ranting about what somebody has done to us. As best we can, we will save rants for another place—even when they are justified—especially since anger may be a trigger for some women in the group. We will focus on our own struggles and share what will promote growth and healing.

5. *Commitment.* Because of our limited time together and the intensity of our subject matter, a strong commitment to attendance is important. If somebody can't make it, she misses the benefits of our time together, and the rest of the group misses the value of shared experiences and insights. In addition to attendance, we commit to praying for each other, no matter where we are in our prayer lives.

6. *Communication.* Please let the group leader and host know if you will be unable to attend. More importantly, as members of a support group, we may freely communicate our needs and prayer requests in the manner determined by the group (e.g., via email or text).

7. *Ownership.* Is there another concern, guideline, or activity we would like to add or discuss to make this group uniquely ours (snacks, fun outings, prayer partners, etc.)?

Appendix B
Response to God's Invitation

God invites us into a personal relationship with Him. If you would like to begin that relationship for the first time or would like to renew it after a long absence, let the following prayer be a guide. Your exact words don't matter, for God knows your heart.

"God, I need You right now more than ever. I've been hurt, and I'm angry. I'm weary, broken, and lost. I need hope. Thank You for showing Your love to me while I am broken. I want to experience more of Your unconditional love and to follow You. I know I've done wrong and can't earn a relationship with You, but Jesus died for my sin, making forgiveness and closeness to You possible. Because of Jesus, I am in Your presence, holy and blameless. Thank You for that amazing gift. Teach me to live for You now, and to regard You as Lord of my life. Amen."

Appendix C .
Further Reflection

The topics covered in *From Broken Vows to Healed Hearts* are brokenness, depression and grief, loneliness, helplessness, fear, guilt, forgiveness, hope, identity, intimacy, joy, and next steps.

Which chapter was the most challenging for me? Why?

In which area have I grown the most over the past few months?

Which devotional do I remember the most and why?

If I were to write a letter from God's point of view, what would He say to me about the past year? What would He say to me about the upcoming year?

In what ways can I continue to grow in my healing and faith?

   Go to church regularly
   Join a small-group Bible study or support group
   Form a support group using this book
   Read back through my journals looking for areas of growth and
      answered prayers
   Commit to regular Bible study and prayer
   Find a safe accountability partner
   Meet with a Christian therapist
   Other: _____

Which of the above do I want to commit to? Who can hold me accountable for this commitment?

Appendix D
Reading Resources

Codependent No More, Melody Beattie

The Gifts of Imperfection: Let Go of Who You Think You're Supposed to Be and Embrace Who You Are, Brené Brown

New Life After Divorce: The Promise of Hope Beyond the Pain, Bill Butterworth

Boundaries in Dating, Henry Cloud

Changes That Heal, Henry Cloud

How to Get a Date Worth Keeping, Henry Cloud

Boundaries: When to Say Yes, How to Say No to Take Control of Your Life, Henry Cloud and John Townsend

Safe People: How to Find Relationships That Are Good for You and Avoid Those That Aren't, Henry Cloud and John Townsend

Give Yourself a Break: Turning Your Inner Critic into a Compassionate Friend, Kim Fredrickson

You're Loved No Matter What: Freeing Your Heart from the Need to Be Perfect, Holley Gerth

Forgiveness: Finding Peace Through Letting Go, Adam Hamilton

Suddenly Single Mom: 52 Messages of Hope, Grace, and Promise, Jeanette Hanscome

Growing Friendships: Connecting More Deeply with Those Who Matter Most, Tracy Klehn

Dancing in the Arms of God: Discover Your Cinderella Story, Connie Neal

Ask It: The Question That Will Revolutionize How You Make Decisions, Andy Stanley

Unglued: Making Wise Choices in the Midst of Raw Emotions, Lysa TerKeurst

Jesus Calling: Enjoying Peace in His Presence, Sarah Young

Appendix E
Support Groups

Celebrate Recovery is a biblical and balanced program that helps you overcome hurts, hang-ups, and habits. It is based on the actual words of Jesus rather than psychological theory. www.celebraterecovery.com

Divorce Care is a divorce recovery support group where you can find help and healing for the hurt of separation and divorce. www.divorcecare.org

New Life Ministries serves people with emotional, spiritual, and relational needs across the nation through radio programs, workshops, and a counseling network. newlife.com

Notes

1. Philip Yancey. *What's So Amazing About Grace?* (Grand Rapids: Zondervan, 1997), 70; emphasis in the original.
2. Connie Neal, *Dancing in the Arms of God: Discover Your Cinderella Story* (self-pub., CreateSpace, 2013), 63.
3. Bob Goff, *Love Does: Discover a Secretly Incredible Life in an Ordinary World* (Nashville: Thomas Nelson, 2012), 46.
4. If you are interested in learning more about the symbolism of a shepherd looking after his sheep, you might read *A Shepherd's Look at Psalm 23* (Grand Rapids: Zondervan, 1970) by W. Phillip Keller, who was a pastor and a shepherd.
5. Philip Yancey, *Where Is God When It Hurts?* (Grand Rapids: Zondervan, 1977), 36.
6. Brené Brown, *Daring Greatly: How the Courage to Be Vulnerable Transforms the Way We Live, Love, Parent, and Lead* (New York: Avery, 2012), 11.
7. Corrie ten Boom, *The Hiding Place* (New York: Bantam Books, 1974), 171.
8. Adam Hamilton, *Forgiveness: Finding Peace Through Letting Go* (Nashville: Abingdon Press, 2012), 115.
9. John and Stasi Eldredge, *Captivating: Unveiling the Mystery of a Woman's Soul* (Nashville: Thomas Nelson, 2010), 120.
10. Joseph T. Hallinan, *Why We Make Mistakes: How We Look Without Seeing, Forget Things in Seconds, and Are All Pretty Sure We Are Way Above Average* (New York: Broadway Books, 2009), 23.

11. Allen Arnold, *The Story of With: A Better Way to Live, Love, and Create* (self-pub., Amazon Digital Services, 2016), 188–89.

12. Arnold, *The Story of With*, 270.

13. Shonda Rhimes, *Year of Yes: How to Dance It Out, Stand in the Sun and Be Your Own Person* (New York: Simon and Schuster, 2015), 296.

Acknowledgments

Nothing is impossible with God, even writing a book. With great gratitude, I thank God for giving me the inspiration and words to share my story, which is really *His* story of love. I see His hand and hear His voice on every page.

I am grateful to many people who believed not only in the message of this book but also in me as I labored to put lessons learned to paper. I have been blessed by their support, love, and inspiration, needing them every step of the way. Without them, my recovery would have been much more difficult, and the writing of this book impossible.

I thank my family, who lovingly supported me throughout the tumultuous divorce process. I offer a special thank-you to my girls, who endured some devastating years and never stopped loving me. I will be forever grateful for the blessings and joy they bring to my life.

I am also grateful for my sister Karen's empathetic words and dispensing of sage advice only when I was ready. My brother, Wayne, was rock steady, always willing and able to help, and my dad's prayerful concern comforted me. Thank you to my nephew, Jarrod Burklow, and his family (Zoe, Jarrod Jr., and Jeffrey) whose open-door policy soothed my soul more than they realize.

God has gifted me with amazing friends whose invaluable hugs, love, and wisdom helped me to move forward. I owe special thanks to several of them: to Elizabeth Kim for all the meals and encouragement; to Valerie Steele, my "I know what you're going through!" sister; to Darlene, for always being available to listen, comfort, and pray; and to April, for her precious friendship and ability to buoy me up to do the seemingly impossible.

Thank you to my fellow creatives in Friends with Pens (Deb Gruelle, Valerie Steele, Elaine Juliusson, Jodie Stevens, and Susan Reynolds), who have shaped my craft and my heart. It's an honor to work together for God's purposes. A special thanks to Deb for her kindred spirit and tireless critiquing before deadlines.

Finally, I thank Rachel Kent at Books and Such and all the amazingly supportive people at Kregel, especially Dawn Anderson for believing in the book and Janyre Tromp for her inspiring ideas. They took a chance on me and helped me every step of the way.

May God bless each of us in our healing journeys.